The Truth of God Incarnate

I0658744

The Truth of God Incarnate

EDITED BY
MICHAEL GREEN

HODDER AND STOUGHTON
LONDON SYDNEY AUCKLAND TORONTO

PUBLISHER'S ACKNOWLEDGMENTS

The sudden interest caused by the publication of *The Myth of God Incarnate* has involved the editor and contributors to this book in great pressure, and special mention must be made of Miss Anne Johnson who typed the manuscript, on occasions far into the night.

Canon Michael Green is Rector of St. Aldate's, Oxford, and was until recently Principal of St. John's College, Nottingham. He is a New Testament scholar, an evangelist, and editor of the 'I Believe' Series.

Bishop Christopher Butler is Auxiliary Bishop to the Archbishop of Westminster and a distinguished Biblical scholar.

Bishop Stephen Neill, an authority on comparative religion, was until recently Professor of Philosophy and Religious Studies at the University of Nairobi.

The Rev. Brian Hebblethwaite is Fellow and Dean of Chapel of Queens' College, Cambridge.

Professor John Macquarrie, Lady Margaret Professor of Divinity at Oxford University, is one of the most influential theologians.

The editor and publisher wish to thank the Editors of *Theology* for their permission to reprint, with slight alterations, the review by Professor John Macquarrie which appears in the September issue of the journal.

Contents

PREFACE: Scepticism in the Church — page 9

1 Jesus in the New Testament *Michael Green* 17

2 Jesus and Myth *Stephen Neill* 58

3 Jesus and History *Stephen Neill* 71

4 Jesus and Later Orthodoxy *Christopher Butler* 89

5 Jesus, God Incarnate *Brian Hebblethwaite* 101

6 Jesus and Historical Scepticism *Michael Green* 107

POSTSCRIPT: Christianity without Incarnation? Some Critical Comments *John Macquarrie* 140

Scepticism in the Church

How MUCH CAN you remove from a car, and still possess what is properly called a car? Lights may be a luxury; you can do without bodywork in warm weather; brakes may be dispensed with, at all events on the level; but if you remove the engine or the chassis it is questionable whether we are still talking about a car at all.

During the past forty-five years we have seen the acceleration of a process which has been going on ever since the eighteenth century, but is now perfectly obvious. We have seen an increasing reluctance to accept traditional full-blooded Christianity, complete with an inspired Bible and an incarnate Christ, and a growing tendency to accommodate Christianity to the spirit of the age. We have seen educated men and women assume that the original article is outmoded, and they have either thrown it away entirely or else modified it drastically. We have seen many theologians engage so wholeheartedly in this process of rejecting some parts of the car and adapting others that we can scarcely believe their protestations that in reality the modernised version runs a lot better than the antiquated original. The process of dismantling the car has been clearly defined and relatively speedy.

First, the doctrine of God's inspiration of Scripture and of its trustworthiness was abandoned. The seeds of this were planted long ago in the days of Lessing; they were watered during the Darwinian controversy at the end of the nineteenth century, and they produced their unambiguous crop of fruit in the arguments against 'fundamentalism' in the nineteen twenties. That same discussion cast doubt on the virgin birth of Jesus Christ; after all, such things do not happen! Next came a rejection of the miracles—or at any rate the nature miracles; as for the healings, we can adduce some sort of psychosomatic parallels, so perhaps there may have been something in them. The Form Criticism of the Gospels which, though strong in Germany since 1918, percolated slowly into Britain, destroyed the assumption that in Mark's Gospel, at any rate, we had a basic, reliable, unadorned piece of history. It appeared that we had nothing of the sort, but a highly theological collection of stories that had originally circulated independently in the mouths of early preachers – and goodness knows how much they may have made up to suit their case.

Many people were shocked at the next stage of the process, the 'death of God' theology associated with men like Altizer in the U.S.A. and the enormous bombshell (so it seemed to many) of *Honest to God* in England. But was it so very surprising? The lights and bodywork had already gone long ago: we were getting near the engine now. In point of fact the 'death of God' school were merely being rather more disingenuous than many of their colleagues; most liberal theologians had ceased to believe in the personal, active God of the Bible, whilst continuing to speak and write about him. The Cheshire cat had disappeared: only the smile remained. In the face of a self-contained, closed scientific universe where there were no more absolutes to be had and where the very idea of miracle was held to be incredible, God talk might remain but God had been withdrawn. I dare say that those who honestly expressed this absence in their published works were amazed at the storm those works provoked: they were, after all, only making explicit what all sensible practitioners of the subject assumed.

There were still two steps to go. The first was to attack the resurrection of Jesus, that supposed bulwark of the supernatural. A whole gamut of books did this in the sixties, many of them breathing a spirit of true devotion, but maintaining that the resurrection never happened – if by that you mean the raising by God of Jesus to a new quality of life which took up and transformed that body which was laid in the tomb on the first Good Friday. And in any case, we were told, it did not matter. The early Christians were not antiquarians pointing to an empty tomb, but enthusiasts full of an Easter faith. The faith was what mattered. To ask what lay behind it was irrelevant and could be represented as quite opposed to the spirit of Christianity; after all, if faith is to be faith, it cannot be propped up by history. The bodily resurrection of Jesus was thus disposed of—not on any new evidence, mark you, but because it was highly antipathetic to the materialistic spirit of the age. Dead men don't rise.

The latest step in the dismantling of the car has been to remove the chassis which held the whole thing together. Most of the men who disbelieved the virgin birth in the thirties and forties still believed that God had come and manifested himself in a unique way in the person of Jesus of Nazareth. The incarnation was still there, quite independent, they would assure us, of the mode in which God chose to involve himself with our flesh. Jesus may well have been the son of Joseph and Mary, but he still brings God into our midst as nobody else does: that is, no doubt, what those early believers long ago were trying to express in their clumsy way by talking of a virgin birth. They were simple folk, didn't understand that these things don't happen, misread the Hebrew of Isaiah 7.14, and produced the incredible story of the virgin birth, following all the pagan parallels of the Hellenistic world in which they lived. All very understandable, and, of course, wrong-headed: but what they were trying to say was correct—that God had visited and redeemed his people in the person of Jesus of Nazareth.

But this half-way house could no longer keep out the rains of scepticism. God (and by that I mean the personal God who acts and intervenes in the affairs of men) is dead: Jesus didn't rise from the dead physically, was not born of a virgin, did not perform miracles—though no doubt he was a remarkable person and his teaching the best the world has seen. But given such assumptions, how could Jesus possibly be the Son of God? How could there be a real incarnation? It is a manner of speaking, a lovely story, like creation and redemption, the virgin birth and the resurrection. It is mythological language, not to be taken ontologically; it is like an Aesop's fable, which nobody in his right mind supposes actually happened as recorded, but which generally points to a fine moral truth. In his article 'Does Christology rest on a mistake?' (*Religious Studies*, 6, pp.69–76) Professor Wiles draws an analogy between traditional language about the incarnation and about the creation. We have to tell two different kinds of story, he maintains: the scientific story of evolution, rejecting the idea of a special act of creation somewhere in the process—and the frankly mythological story about the spirit of God moving on the face of the waters and so on. He advocates weaving the two stories together in poetically creative ways, but not binding them together at some specific point. So with the incarnation. He wants to tell a human story of "the partial overcoming in human lives of that repudiation of the fellowship with God of which the doctrine of the fall speaks". And then there is the "mythological story of God's total self-giving". What we must not do is to tie the two stories together by claiming that at one particular point—namely the life, death and resurrection of Jesus of Nazareth—the two stories are literally united with each other. Do you see what is happening? The mythological story is fine so long as it stays upstairs, so to speak, and does not come down into the living room. We live in the living room—and only go upstairs in order to dream when the process of living has become too exhausting and depressing to endure.

That is the situation we are at, just now. Recently the B.B.C. has put out a film entitled 'Who was Jesus?', made by a Cambridge theologian, the Revd. Don Cupitt. The figure of Jesus was as tenuous in this presentation as the photography was splendid. A lovely story. But did he really rise? Did he really do miracles? Was he really born of a virgin? Was he really Son of God? The answer to all these questions was a sophisticated 'No'. And to show that Mr. Cupitt was backed up by the Religious Department of the B.B.C. in this presentation, it is perhaps worth recording that the 'orthodox' comments from believing scholars which they filmed as a commentary on the programme were in fact excised before the programme went out. It is clear that we are not dealing with the extravagances of a John Allegro with his mushroom myth, or the artistic agnosticism of a Tim Rice with his Superstar, but with a view of the Christian gospel widely held within influential positions of the Church itself.

This has been made abundantly clear by the publication of a series of essays edited by John Hick, *The Myth of God Incarnate* (S.C.M., 1977). I asked a friend who he thought would have written a book with such a title. He replied, "The Communists." This could well have been correct: it is official Communist propaganda that the Jesus of the Gospels is a second-century mythical figure created to account for a movement of the masses which, they believe, Christianity was in its earliest days. But no. The authors of this book are theologians, clergymen for the most part. If it seems to you that the title of the present book might owe something to the S.C.M. title, you are quite right. We have written the present book because we are concerned at the impression which *The Myth of God Incarnate* is likely to make in the minds of many who regard the word 'mythical' as synonymous with 'untrue'. In point of fact, the authors of this symposium use the word 'myth' in a variety of ways, as we shall point out. But when responsible theologians use a technical word in such a way as the title and main selling point of their book, then they have ceased to be academic speculators and have turned into propagandists.

There are two appropriate actions one can take to propaganda. One can wait for it to die away: truth tends to prevail in the end. The Ark of the Lord does not need human hands to prop it up every time it is jolted. On the other hand one can take the propaganda on in direct discussion, see how well based it is, and let the rights and wrongs emerge.

We have chosen the latter course for a number of reasons. We believe that it is high time for those who do not accept a reductionist Christology to stand up and be counted. We believe that the presuppositions behind the current scepticism are not compelling, and that the implications of it are very far-reaching and corroding. And we believe that a response from a variety of theological and cultural backgrounds such as we represent will sufficiently show that a repudiation of the sort of position most recently evidenced in *The Myth of God Incarnate* is not the concern of a mere conservative backlash, but is broadly based in the Church.

Although we have deliberately slanted our book towards *The Myth of God Incarnate*, we are not concerned with a detailed discussion of the bewildering and incompatible theological positions it embodies, but with the broader issues which a book like this highlights. The book itself was written by scholars and presumably for scholars; it is likely to prove somewhat indigestible for the general public.

It is doubtful whether it is a book which will greatly enhance the reputation of its authors, except, perhaps, that of Frances Young who writes with discipline and balance. But what are we to make of Professor Hick who announces in his essay that he used the word 'myth' to mean "a story which is told but which is not literally true" (p.178) and then uses it in his Introduction in an entirely different sense: "Orthodoxy is a myth" (p.x), and in yet a third sense when claiming in that same Introduction that the conception of Jesus as God incarnate is "mythological or poetic"? Is orthodoxy poetic? When 'myth' is used in so indisciplined a manner, Professor Wiles' statement that, "If what held Christians together were seen as the use of the same myths rather than holding the same beliefs, it might be easier for Christians to accept the measure of variety that there both should and will be between them" (p.164) becomes almost amusing. And if high-grade entertainment is what you are looking for, I recommend Michael Goulder's chapter on 'Two roots of the Christian myth' which sets out to persuade us that incarnational speculations were introduced into the Church by Simon Magus. If anyone set out to put forward conservative conclusions on the sort of basis adopted in that essay and in other parts of this book, he would be laughed out of court, and justly. Indeed, Frances Young has said all that needs to be said of it: "the supposed parallels can be regarded as hypothetical reconstructions in the minds of modern scholars, corresponding to no historical reality" (p.103).

I very much doubt whether the publication of this book will enhance the reputation of S.C.M. Publishers either. One can get away with an *Honest to God* once in a while. But to follow it with a book like *The Myth of God Incarnate*, extensively publicised and launched at a press conference, is likely in the long run to be counterproductive. The authors are well aware that "the popular understanding of myth today is of something delusive . . . a kind of mirage, something that leads people astray" (p.164), and yet a religious publishing house is prepared to put it out under the title of *The Myth of God Incarnate*.

CHAPTER ONE

Jesus in the New Testament

MICHAEL GREEN

WE KNOW VERY little about Jesus of Nazareth apart from
the Gospels and Epistles which go to make up our New
Testament. If, therefore, we are to make up our minds
whether the incarnation of God in Jesus of Nazareth is a
fact or a myth, we must begin with the New Testament,
not with any speculative theories spun out by theologians
in the fourth century—or the twentieth. What evidence does
the New Testament afford on so momentous a matter?

It offers a great deal. So much, that it will be quite
impossible to do more than outline the main thrust of it in
this chapter. So much, that libraries are filled with books
on the subject—and the most recent, Professor C. F. D.
Moule's *Origin of Christology*, is likely to prove one of the
best. It is probable that if his book had been available a
year ago *The Myth of God Incarnate* would not have seen
the light of day. In contrast to Professor Moule's detailed
work, the symposium is weak in its handling of New Testament evidence. Michael Goulder astonishingly attributes belief in the deity of Christ to the supposed influence
of Simon Magus on the Church, and also to the psy-
chological impact of Peter's experience of the (mythical!)
resurrection, and the subsequent "power of hysteria
within a small community". The other contributor on the
New Testament evidence, Frances Young, gives us a careful examination of the background, Jewish and pagan, for

the idea of deity incarnate in a human being. She has the honesty to conclude that there is no complete analogy to the total Christian claim about Jesus in pre-Christian material, and that all partial analogies are inadequate (p.118f). It is surprising therefore to find Professor Hick airily claiming the support of Frances Young for his assertion that "there is nothing in the least surprising in the deification of Jesus in that cultural environment"—a conclusion which her careful examination of the evidence does little to support. He goes on to find it "natural and intelligible that Jesus should come to be hailed as son of God, and that later this poetry should have hardened into prose, and escalated from a metaphorical son of God to a metaphysical God the Son" (p.176). Let us examine some of the New Testament assertions themselves, and make up our own minds whether their authors intended them to be taken as poetry or prose, as myth or as sober fact.

I. THE SPREAD OF THE NEW TESTAMENT TESTIMONY

The claims of St. Paul

Let us begin with Saul of Tarsus. That redoubtable opponent of the Christian cause first regarded it as a blasphemous heresy, but was converted and became its greatest missionary. His first extant letters, to the Thessalonians, date from A.D. 50 or 51. This is how he speaks of Jesus: first he welcomes the Church as being 'in' God the Father and the Lord Jesus Christ, and remembers how they "turned to God from idols to serve the living and true God and to wait for his Son from heaven, whom he raised from the dead, Jesus who delivers us from the wrath to come" (1.1, 10). The return of Jesus Christ on the Day of Judgment is identified with the Day of the Lord which the Old Testament prophets expected (4.15–5.2). God will complete our sanctification at the coming of the Lord Jesus Christ.

In his second letter, written a few months later, he speaks of the judgment that is to fall on "those who do not know God and do not obey the gospel of our Lord Jesus" (1.8). This will fall when not only God but the Lord Jesus "is revealed from heaven with his mighty angels" (1.7). Meanwhile, when he prays that "God may make you worthy of his call" it is "so that the name of our Lord Jesus may be glorified in you" (1.12). And so we could go on. In these earliest letters, written some twenty years after the resurrection, we find Paul struggling for words in which to describe the association of Jesus with God in grace, glory, salvation and judgment. Already we have a story "which co-stars Jesus and God" as Dennis Nineham rather indelicately puts it (p.202). And all this is before Paul had been corrupted by the incarnational theology of Simon Magus!

Paul's letters to Corinth were penned in the mid-fifties. This is how he refers to Jesus in 1 Corinthians 8.6: "To us there is one God, the Father, from whom are all things and for whom we exist, and one Lord Jesus Christ, through whom are all things and through whom we exist"—and this, mark you, in a passage where he is insisting that in contrast to the Hellenistic world (where there are many 'gods' and 'lords') "there is no God but one". Is this merely the poetic language which Dr. Hick would have us see? It is hard to suppose so, in the light of such claims as 2 Corinthians 4.4 where Paul refers to the "light of the gospel of the glory of Christ who is the image of God", or his closing words "the grace of our Lord Jesus Christ, and the love of God and the fellowship of the Holy Spirit be with you all" (2 Cor. 13.14). It is interesting to note, in passing, that the concept of the Trinity, far from being a late invention, is firmly based in the New Testament itself. It is evident in the passage we have just looked at; it is there in 1 Corinthians 12.4–6: "Now there are varieties of gifts, but the same Spirit. And there are varieties of service, but the same Lord. And there are varieties of working, but it is the same God who inspires them all in every one." In his Letter to the Ephesians Paul refers to the Trinity no less than four times. In 2.18 he speaks of our having access through Christ and by the activity of the one Spirit to the Father. In 2.22 he speaks of the collaboration of the Trinity in building up the Christian Church: "In Christ you are built together for a place for God to dwell through the Spirit." In 3.14–17 he prays to the Father that they may be strengthened by the Spirit in the inner man, that Christ may make his home in their hearts. And in speaking of Christian fundamentals in 4.4–6 Paul can assume one Lord, one Spirit, one God and Father of all. Fascinating, is it not, that Professor Hick can suppose that this trinitarian concept springs from a pre-critical acceptance of the Fourth Gospel reports of Jesus' teaching as historical? These writings of St. Paul precede by half a century the date when, on Dr. Hick's supposition, the Fourth Gospel was written!

There remain two important passages in St. Paul's writings at which we must at least glance before we move on to other areas of New Testament witness. The first is the Epistle to the Colossians. Paul is countering a syncretising heresy in which Jesus is put alongside other mediators as just one of the ways to God—a similar position to that which Professor Hick advocates in his paper, maintaining as he does that other great world faiths are also, at their best, ways of salvation (p.182). Paul denies this strongly (Col. 1.15f). He lumps together the so-called mediators between God and man which these Colossians espoused and asserts that "the image of the God we cannot see" is found in "his beloved Son" alone. He is "the firstborn of all creation" ('firstborn', a fascinating word with a complex history, had long ceased to be used exclusively in its literal sense and came to denote priority in rank as well as in time—cf. Psalm 89.27). Paul leaves us in no doubt what he means by the word, "for by him were all things created". Not only is Christ the source of creation; but he is the goal of the whole universe. "All things were created for him." As if that were not enough, Paul has so clear a grasp of the cosmic significance of Jesus the Messiah that he adds "by him all things hang together". He is the principle of coherence in the universe! It is he who is the head of the Christian body, the Church. It is he who is the firstborn from the dead, the pledge of the Christian's destiny. In everything he is pre-eminent. "In him," continues the writer, "all the fullness of God was pleased to dwell." Now that is highly significant. The 'fullness' was a technical term used by the heretics at Colossae to describe the totality of the superhuman intermediaries they reverenced. Paul boldly asserts that this 'fullness' of divine attributes does not reside in a multiplicity of mediators but in one alone, Jesus. He makes the point again with immense force in 2.9. "In him the whole fullness of deity dwells bodily."

Greek is a very sensitive and expressive language, and Paul employs all the nuances available to him in order to express his conviction of the full deity of Jesus. We have already met the idea of 'fullness'. He denies that God's fullness is spread around among a variety of mediators, be they "thrones or dominions or principalities or authorities" (in so far as they have any reality at all, these forces were created by Christ and for him, 1.16). The 'fullness' rests in Christ alone. Greek has two words for 'live' or 'have your home'. The weaker one suggests that your abode is temporary; you may move on. He does not use this word, *paroikein*, but the much stronger word, *katoikein*, which means to "make your permanent abode". The fullness of deity has its permanent location in Jesus. Moreover, Greek has two words for 'deity', one very much weaker, like our 'divine' which can be applied to a hero or even a dancing partner! In recent years some New Testament theologians have gone overboard in searching for examples of the 'divine man', *theios aner*. But it is not this attenuated sense of the word 'deity' that St. Paul uses.

He goes for the stronger, unambiguous word, *theotēs*, meaning Godhead. The fullness of the Godhead makes its permanent home in Jesus. Such is his claim. And lest we might be tempted to take this daring metaphysical claim in a weakened, poetic sense, such as the authors of *The Myth of God Incarnate* invite us to, Paul adds a devastating final word, utterly outrageous to Greek and Jew alike, *somatikōs*. It means 'bodily'. He is claiming as powerfully as words will allow that the inconceivable has taken place, and that Almighty God has made his permanent home in Jesus of Nazareth; not in some 'Christ idea' or 'Christ myth' but in the human and exalted Christ Jesus the Lord (Paul gives him his full title, 2.6). It is difficult to imagine how anyone could have found words more clear and decisive. Paul may have been wrong; it is hard to claim that he is merely being 'poetic'.

The final passage we shall look at is Philippians 2.4–11. It gives us a profound insight into what Paul meant when he applied the title 'Lord' to Jesus. The word itself, *kyrios*, could mean anything from 'sir' to 'God Almighty'. How are we to understand it when applied to Jesus? This passage gives the answer. It is almost universally understood in New Testament circles to be an early Christian hymn to Christ which Paul takes over and uses to reinforce his plea to the Philippians for humility. The reason for this view is that, not only are many of the words in these verses un-Pauline, but it is not difficult to retranslate the whole thing back into Aramaic poetry. This suggests that it is very old, and comes from the earliest stratum of the Aramaic-speaking church. We find in this amazing early piece of worship to Jesus a combination of three of the highest of Old Testament motifs. He is the Son of Man, colleague of the Ancient of Days according to Daniel 7.13. He is the suffering Servant of the Lord, who bears the sins of the world according to Isaiah 53 (and the link between Isa. 53.12 and Phil. 2.7 is particularly strong). And supremely he takes the place of God Almighty in the Old

Testament, as the one to whom every knee will bow and every tongue confess. Is it not perfectly astonishing that within a few years of the death of this wandering rabbi Jesus, his followers should be ransacking the Old Testament for titles to do justice to his person and significance, and should settle on one which involved universal worship and loyalty, the name of God himself? That is the name above every name. That is the name conferred on Jesus. That is what lies behind 'Lord' when attributed to him. He is identified with Almighty God who had said in Isaiah 45.22f, "I am God and there is no other. By myself I have sworn, 'To me every knee shall bow and every tongue shall swear'." Mere poetry, do you think?

Of course, such a claim does not mean that God Almighty has abdicated in favour of his Son. It means that the Son shares the Father's nature, and that the God to whom universal worship will be given is the one who has disclosed himself as Jesus. It would be ridiculous to imagine that Jesus is God, *tout simple*. The New Testament writers do not claim this for him; they know he is very much one of us. But they do insist that he is not just one of us. He is, so to speak, the window into God. That is no doubt why Paul insists that before the incarnation Jesus Christ shared the very form of God: "who, being in the form of God, did not account equality with God a thing to be grasped". That is another very careful piece of writing. There are two Greek words which express the participle 'being'. The weaker is *ōn*; the stronger, *huparchōn* (meaning 'being from the beginning'). It is the latter which Paul uses when he says that Jesus had always been in the 'form' of God. Likewise 'form' has two Greek words which do duty for it. There is the word *schēma* which indicates the external appearance, whether or not it corresponds exactly to the inner reality. Paul does not use that word. Instead, he chooses the stronger word, *morphē*, which indicates the outer form while implying that it gives precise expression to the inner reality. So the meaning of this amazingly profound 'hymn' to Christ in Philippians 2 is this, in a nutshell. It means that Jesus had always been one with God; that he voluntarily laid aside those aspects of his deity that would have been impossible to combine with sharing our human condition; that he became one of us, shared our death, even death on a cross. And that the Father has openly bestowed on him the sacred name of God, for it is to the divine love and judgment as brought to us by God-become-flesh that every knee will eventually bow. A mind-boggling claim! But that is what the earliest Christians believed. That is what the Aramaic-speaking church believed, and formulated into a hymn or confessional statement many years before Paul wrote his letter to the Philippians (about A.D. 60, or possibly five years earlier). In the face of this, to argue that the full deity of Christ was only gradually asserted after decades had rolled by is not only inaccurate, it is very bad scholarship. Jesus was accorded this status by his followers from the earliest days of the Christian church.

I have spent a lot of time on Paul because he is probably the earliest writer we have in the New Testament. He wrote between twenty and thirty years after the crucifixion. He puts us in touch with the beliefs of the earliest Christians. But the really impressive thing is the way in which this conviction of Paul is to be found everywhere you turn in the New Testament. There is no substantial difference between the various writers, despite the fact that they wrote independently of one another, and in different parts of the Empire. They are all convinced of the deity of their Lord Jesus.

The claims of the evangelists

Each of the four evangelists makes plain his conviction in his own way. Mark, the earliest, heads his work "The beginning of the Gospel of Jesus Christ, the Son of God" (1.1), and at once introduces a trinitarian motif in the story of the Baptism of Jesus, where the voice of the Father and the coming of the Spirit combine to assure Jesus (and the reader) that "Thou art my beloved Son in whom I am well pleased". Matthew is at pains to draw attention to the significance of Jesus' name which means "Yahweh is the Saviour" (1.21) and to the fact that his coming means 'Emmanuel', 'God is with us' (1.23).

Luke introduces Jesus with these words, "He will be great, and will be called the Son of the Most High; and the Lord God will give him the throne of his father David, and he will reign over the house of Jacob for ever, and of his kingdom there shall be no end ... The Holy Spirit will come upon you", so runs the message to Mary his mother, "and the power of the Most High will overshadow you; therefore the child to be born will be called holy, the Son of God" (1.32–35). It might look as though the allusion to his inheriting David's kingdom was a contradiction to the theme of divine Sonship, but such is not the case. One of the most interesting discoveries among the Dead Sea Scrolls is a collection of texts which the men of Qumran applied to their hopes of an Ultimate Deliverer. One of those texts was 2 Samuel 7.11–14. God promises David that "The Lord will make you a house ... I will raise up your offspring after you, who shall come forth from your body [*as Jesus did on his mother Mary's side*] and I will establish his kingdom. He shall build a house for my name, and I will establish the throne of his kingdom for ever. [*This actually happened in the case of Jesus. But of what earthly ruler could this be said?*] I will be his Father and he shall be my Son." Son of David through his mother, then, on the human plane. But Son of God on another plane. Luke is aware that the divine Sonship is veiled during his earthly ministry. It breaks out, however, all over the pages of the Acts. He would have agreed with the old Christological formula which we find in Romans 1.3: "His Son was descended from David according to the flesh, and designated [or defined] Son of God in power according to the Spirit of holiness by his resurrection from the dead."

St. John is the most explicit of all, as has long been recognised. "The Word" is his philosophical term for Jesus. It recalled God's creative word or *fiat* in Genesis; his revelatory 'word of the Lord' through the prophets; the Old Testament revelation which was almost accorded an independent personality in Proverbs; the universal principle of rationality so dear to Philo and the Stoics—all this and much more lay behind this mysterious title he attributes to Jesus, "the Word". But the status of this Word is beyond question. He was in the beginning with God. He is the principle of life. He is the agent in creation. He is the light of the world. And he is God. Here again the Greek is so careful. It does not use the definite article, *ho theos*, as if Jesus exhaustively defined the deity; but the simple *theos*, indicating that Jesus shared the very nature of God but did not exhaustively embody him. It leaves room, in other words, for the Father who sent him.

St. John then declares what no Greek philosopher, no Hebrew prophet would ever have dared to say about anyone—that the Word, this incomparably superior being who shared God's life, his creativity and his very nature—became flesh and lived among us. It is a definitive claim that in the confines of a human life (a life they knew well) the Ultimate had become embodied, the Absolute had become contemporary. It was the philosophical claim for the deity of Christ. And when St. John goes on in 1.18 to say "No one has ever seen God; the only Son [or as the best manuscripts read, 'the only begotten one, himself God'] has made him known" he is making the point in equally emphatic though less philosophical terms. Throughout the Gospel we find that Jesus "called God his Father, making himself equal with God" (5.18). We are, therefore well prepared for Thomas' confession at the end of the Gospel, "My Lord and my God" (20.28). After all, the author explicitly states that he has chosen to record incidents from the life of Jesus which will lead his readers to "believe that Jesus is the Christ, the Son of God" (20.31). The evangelist believed it. He wanted others to believe it too.

The claims of other New Testament writers

One of the oldest parts of the Gospels is the material known as Q, a substantial body of sayings of Jesus recorded in Matthew and Luke but absent from Mark. Does the Q material embody this amazing claim to deity which we find in the Gospels as a whole? Yes it does. Let us take as an example the remarkable passage, found in Matthew 11.25ff and Luke 10.21ff, where Jesus claims an exclusive relationship with the Father. He maintains that he alone knows the Father. He alone can introduce men to the Father. To him alone the Father has delivered all things. Let men therefore come to him. "All things have been delivered to me by my Father; and no one knows the Son except the Father, and no one knows the Father except the Son and anyone to whom the Son chooses to reveal him. Come to me, all who labour and are heavy laden, and I will give you rest." What religious leader has ever spoken like that? These are the words of one who can point to himself with both humility and authority because he does in fact constitute the meeting point of God and man.

I do not want to labour the point. Wherever you look in the New Testament you find this same conviction that in Jesus God has expressed himself personally. The little Epistle of Jude can equate "perverting the grace of our God in licentiousness" with "denying our only Master and Lord, Jesus Christ" (1.4), and gives clear trinitarian teaching in 1.20,21. The Book of Revelation makes the same point in its own strange imagery. The Lamb occupies one throne with God (22.3) and receives the worship of believers precisely as does his Father: "Worthy is the Lamb who was slain, to receive power and wealth and wisdom and might and honour and glory and blessing."

John continues: "And I heard every creature in heaven and on earth and in the sea, and all therein, saying, 'To him who sits upon the throne and to the Lamb be blessing and honour and glory and might for ever and ever' ", and "the elders fell down and worshipped" (5.13ff).

But before we leave this sketchy survey of the New Testament evidence two passages are particularly worthy of mention. The first is Peter's sermon on the Day of Pentecost, because the authors of *The Myth of God Incarnate* are particularly partial to its description of Jesus as "a man attested to you by God" (2.22). Does this point to a primitive and non-supernaturalist Christology as Messrs. Goulder and Hick suppose? I am gratified that they should accord such reliability to the speeches in Acts, normally considered by scholars of their persuasion to be late Lucan fabrications. But their argument will not bear critical inspection for a moment. That same speech of Peter's maintains that the Father has exalted Jesus to the right hand of God, that he is the fulfilment of Psalms 110.1 in which Yahweh calls him 'Lord', and the promise "And it shall be that whosoever calls on the name of the Lord [i.e. Yahweh in Joel 2.32] shall be saved" is explained thus: "Repent, and be baptised every one of you in the name of Jesus Christ for the forgiveness of sins" (Acts 2.21,34,38). The name of Yahweh is the name of Jesus. It is clear that we cannot give too high significance to the titles with which the sermon ends, "Let all the house of Israel therefore know assuredly that God has made him both Lord and Christ, this Jesus whom you crucified" (2.36).

Finally, a glance at the beginning of the Epistle to the Hebrews, written by some unknown Christian about the year A.D. 66. "In many and various ways God spoke of old to our fathers by the prophets; but in these last days he has spoken to us by a Son." So far so good; is this metaphorical language? See how he goes on. "Him he has appointed the heir of all things; through him also he created the world. He reflects the glory of God and bears the very stamp of his nature, upholding the universe by his word of power." In other words, Jesus is God's final and personal message to man: beyond him, God has nothing more to say. He is the one for whom the whole world exists. He is the one who fashioned it. He sustains the whole universe. He reflects the nature of God (the Greek original hints that he does so as closely as sunshine reflects the sun). He bears the stamp of God's character (and the original hints that he does so as precisely as marks in the wax reflect the seal that made them). Such is the conviction of the writer to the Hebrews. Such is, in essence (however variously expressed) the conviction of all the New Testament writers. They had come to the conclusion that in a unique, personal way, "God was in Christ". This was no exaggeration, no hyperbole, mythology or poetic licence. They meant it to be taken with the utmost seriousness. They believed in the truth of God incarnate.

2. THE VARIETY OF THE NEW TESTAMENT TESTIMONY

Titles given to Jesus

It is, I think, a fair criticism of the way in which Christology has developed down the centuries, to say that undue emphasis has been laid on the 'Son' as a Christological title. It is, after all, analogical language; what other language can one use of God? It is moreover, wide open to misinterpretation as though it implied that God begets sons in the same way as we do. And it is only one of the categories in which the New Testament sees Jesus. So let us broaden the discussion.

The breadth of titles accorded to Jesus is startling. They see him as the Messiah or Christ; that is to say, the culmination of Jewish hopes for deliverance and the inaugurator of the final days of salvation. So central was this understanding of him at any rate in Jewish-Christian circles, that in many of the books of the New Testament 'Christ' almost appears as a surname for Jesus of Nazareth.

They see him as the Son of Man. This is a fascinating phrase which meets us in the Psalms (8 and 80), in Ezekiel (frequently being used of the prophet himself) and in Daniel. Jesus himself alludes to the Daniel passage (7.13) where the Son of Man comes to the Ancient of Days and is given a kingdom and power and glory. He does so most strikingly at his trial where he tells his judges that men will see him, the Son of Man, sitting on the right hand of power and coming in the clouds of heaven (Mark 14.62). An enormous literature has gathered around this title. It is exceedingly complex. But there can be little doubt that in Daniel, and the use of it made by Jesus at his trial, the Son of Man indicates a supernatural figure of power and glory who stands on God's side of the great divide rather than man's. At the same time the human strand of the Son of Man in the Psalms and the prophetic element found in Ezekiel are not missing in Jesus' use of the title for himself. There was the added attraction that the title had not been used in Judaism as a focus for militaristic (and misleading) messianic hopes as 'Messiah' had been, and it had a delightful ambivalence like the French *on* or the German *man* which could enable it to be used either as a designation of oneself or of somebody else. The Book of Enoch, which may or may not be pre-Christian, also employs the title widely, and presents us with a Son of Man who is the highest imaginable being under God, and who shares his powers in the saving and the judging of mankind.

Another great title was 'the prophet like Moses', derived from Deuteronomy 18.15: "The Lord your God will raise up for you a prophet like me from among you, from your brethren—him you shall heed." The model was particularly apt, for Moses had been God's agent both in revelation and redemption. So some New Testament writers used this title of Jesus, whom they saw as the ultimate in revelation and redemption alike (cf. Acts 3.22f, 7.37).

One of the most sublime chapters in the Old Testament, Isaiah 53, speaks of a suffering servant of God who would bear the sins of the people, make intercession for the transgressors, and make many to be accounted righteous. The followers of Jesus were quite sure that this destiny had been fulfilled in the death and resurrection of their Master and they applied it to him freely (e.g. 1 Peter 2.22ff, Luke 22.37, Acts 8.32f, Hebrews 9.28).

The Old Testament had looked to a day when God would establish a New Covenant between himself and man, not like "the covenant which they broke, though I was a husband to them, says the Lord. But this is the covenant which I will make with the House of Israel after those days, says the Lord. I will put my law within them, and I will write it upon their hearts, and I will be their God and they shall be my people. And no longer shall each man teach his neighbour and his brother saying 'Know the Lord', for they shall all know me, from the least of them to the greatest, says the Lord, for I will forgive their iniquity and I will remember their sin no more" (Jeremiah 31.31ff). Jesus claimed to fulfil this prophecy. He referred to it as he instituted the Eucharist during his Last Supper with the Twelve (Matt. 26.26ff) and the Christians were confident that he had triumphantly achieved his claim. He had interiorised God's demands within their hearts; he had given them a personal knowledge of the Lord; he had forgiven their sins. The New Covenant had replaced the Old. It is a major theme in the Epistle to the Hebrews (chs. 8 and 10).

A similar hope was that the Spirit of the Lord, who had been restricted to few and special people in Old Testament days, would be made available to all God's people in the days of salvation. For this men longed, and all the more so in the centuries immediately prior to the Christian era. The rabbis tell us how keenly the people of Israel were aware that God's Spirit was absent from their midst. Ezekiel had prophesied "A new heart will I give you, and a new spirit will I put within you; and I will take out of your flesh the heart of stone, and give you a heart of flesh. And I will put my Spirit within you, and cause you to walk in my statutes and be careful to observe my ordinances" (Ezekiel 36.26ff). Isaiah, too had known that the day would come when "a shoot shall come forth out of the stump of Jesse, and a branch shall grow out of his roots. And the Spirit of the Lord shall rest upon him, the Spirit of wisdom and understanding, the Spirit of counsel and might, the Spirit of knowledge and the fear of the Lord" (11.1ff). Well, as all the Gospels bear testimony, the disciples saw Jesus as the man baptised with the Spirit, the one on whom the Spirit rested, the one who could impart him to others. That is the meaning of the Baptism and of the Farewell Discourses in St. John's Gospel. And the Christians were sure that the Spirit of the Lord, long promised, embodied in Jesus of Nazareth, was resident within their own lives. They could therefore speak equally about the Spirit of God and the Spirit of Christ: they referred to the same person. Thus in Romans 8.9–11 Paul can ring the changes of nomenclature without embarrassment: "You are in the Spirit, if the Spirit of God dwells in you. Anyone who does not have the Spirit of Christ does not belong to him ... If the Spirit of him who raised up Jesus from the dead dwells in you ..." The Spirit of God and the Spirit of Jesus are one.

In the previous section we looked at other titles of Jesus, such as 'Lord' and 'Word', 'The Glory of God' and so forth. If space allowed we could investigate others. The point which I want to emphasise is that in every instance the Christians ransack the Old Testament (the recognised locus of revelation) for the highest titles and concepts available, and then apply them one and all to a man they had known and followed and seen die; a man they were confident was risen and alive. Such a procedure is unparalleled in the history of the world. By contrast, the interpretation of Scripture in such a way that all these symbols and figures for the 'greatest' were believed to converge on a single historical figure, was utterly new and startling. It took Jesus of Nazareth to precipitate it. Those who knew him strained the bounds of language in order to point out who he was—and is.

Implicit assumptions about Jesus

But perhaps the most impressively varied evidence comes not in any titles at all (though New Testament research has concentrated to an abnormal degree on such titles in recent years), but in the implicit indications as to who Jesus is, which lie buried just beneath the surface of the New Testament. What I mean is this. Predicates and functions attributed to God in the Old Testament are taken over and used of Christ in the New— quite naturally and unostentatiously. Let us look at some of them, and ask ourselves afresh whether these men could have used language in this way if they intended to give us merely a poetic or mythical interpretation of the deity of Christ.

In the Old Testament God alone is 'the redeemer'. "For with Yahweh is steadfast love and plenteous redemption, and he will ransom Israel from all his iniquities" (Ps. 130.7). This is clearly God's prerogative. But what do we find on the first page of the New Testament? "You shall call his name Jesus, for he will save his people from their sins" (Matt. 1.21). What God alone could do, Jesus was about to accomplish! Titus 2.13 takes up the point: "Our great God and Saviour Jesus Christ gave himself for us that he might ransom us from all iniquity." Both God's role and his name are taken over by Jesus in the work of redemption. Had he not claimed that this is precisely what he came into our world to do? (Mark 10.45).

T—B

In the Old Testament 'glory' belongs to God alone. It is the effulgence of his presence viewed under the imagery of light. Isaiah 42.8 reads "I am Yahweh, and I shall not give my glory to another" and it is repeated in 48.11. But what does Jesus say in the famous prayer of John 17? "And now glorify me, Father, with the glory which I had with thee before the world was made" (v.5). Paul can write, "Had they known it, they would not have crucified the Lord of glory" (1 Cor. 2.8) and elsewhere he speaks of the "glory of Christ who is the image of God" (2 Cor. 4.4). And James describes Jesus as "the Lord of glory" (2.1).

In the Old Testament it is the word of God which endures for ever, in contrast to the flower which fades (Isa. 40.8), and Jesus clearly accepted and taught this view of the Old Testament as authoritative divine revelation. His words in Matthew 5.18 make this abundantly plain: "For truly I say to you, till heaven and earth pass away, not an iota, not a dot will pass from the law." Yet he makes just the same claim for his own words, "Heaven and earth will pass away, but my words will not pass away" (Mark 13.31). His words, like the words of Yahweh, are eternal. Such is the claim.

There are many other such concepts applied to Yahweh in the Old Testament and taken over and applied to Jesus in the New. We have already seen how the name of Yahweh to which every knee should bow and whom every tongue should confess (Isa. 42.23) becomes the name of Jesus (Phil. 2.10f). It is just the same with images like the 'Shepherd of Israel', transferred from Yahweh (Psalm 23.1, Ezek. 34.15) to Jesus (John 10.11, 1 Pet. 5.4, Heb. 13.20). So is 'the Bridegroom'. In the Old Testament it is Yahweh who is the bridegroom or husband of his people (Hosea 2.16, Isa. 62.5), but in the New Testament we find this to be the role of Jesus (Mark 2.19, Matt. 25.1–13) and in the last vision of the Apocalypse we find the church awaiting Christ's return "like a bride adorned for her husband". In the Old Testament it is

Yehweh who is the 'Saviour' (e.g. Isa. 43.3, 45.21): "There is no other God beside me, a righteous God and a Saviour. Turn to me and be saved, all the ends of the earth, for I am God and there is none else." But in the New Testament we find that Jesus frequently bears the title Saviour. "Whosoever shall call upon the name of the Lord shall be saved" we read in Joel 2.32; but when it is quoted by Paul in Romans 10.13 it is applied to Jesus and so, incidentally, is the "he who believes on him will not be confounded" (Rom. 10.11 quoting Isa. 28.16 where it indicates Yahweh).

But perhaps the most striking places of all are those in which Jesus is called the 'Judge'. If any function belongs to God alone, this must be it. And the Old Testament is in no doubt about it. "I will sit to judge all the nations," says Yahweh (Joel 3.12). But in Matthew 25.31ff we read that Jesus will occupy the throne of glory (and there can be none greater than that) and preside at the Last Judgment. In that day it will be he who distinguishes between those who have merely said "Lord, Lord" and those who have actually done the will of his heavenly Father. For him to say "I never knew you; depart from me, you evildoers" will suffice for their ultimate destiny. Could any words be plainer? Is it surprising that 2 Timothy speaks of "Jesus Christ who shall judge the living and the dead"? Or that Paul does not distinguish between the "judgment seat of God" and the "judgment seat of Christ" (Rom. 14.10, 2 Cor. 5.10)?

The list could be greatly extended, but enough has been said to show that not merely in their titles and attestations, but in the quiet assumptions of the functions they applied to him, the early Christians saw Jesus as no mere man, but the one who shared the nature of God Almighty. And that is why they gave him worship.

3. THE REASON FOR THIS NEW TESTAMENT TESTIMONY

We have seen reason to believe that when the New Testament writers ascribe deity to Jesus they did not mean it in any attenuated, mythical or poetic sense. They meant what they said: that God had visited and redeemed his people, and that he had done so in and through Jesus. We must now ask whether there was any precedent for so astonishing a claim. Was there something in the Jewish or Hellenistic background of these early believers which allowed them to speak in such terms of a fellow human being? Was it comparatively easy for them to believe in the divinity of Jesus because of the cultural heritage which was theirs?

Hellenistic parallels to the deity of Christ?

Let us begin with the Hellenistic world. At first sight there are lots of parallels to the incarnation, death and resurrection of Jesus in the myths of Apollo and Asclepius, Hercules and Tammuz. The mystery cults, the cycle of the year and of human life: these provide all the parallels we need. What if Jesus was called 'Lord' by his followers? So was Serapis. What if he was said to be born of a virgin? So were half the members of the pantheon. What if he was supposed to have ascended to heaven? So was Hercules, raised thereby to the rank of divinity; and so were the Roman Emperors after their decease (it all began when somebody claimed that he had seen a new star arise from Julius Caesar's funeral pyre!). What was so very special about Jesus?

The really special thing was this: nobody had ever attributed divinity and a virgin birth, resurrection and ascension to a *historical person* whom lots of people knew. And certainly nobody claimed that the one and only God, the creator and judge of the whole earth, had embodied himself in Apollo, Hercules, Augustus, and the rest. Folk like Apollo were mythical figures whom nobody in their right mind believed in; but they were there in Homer—it was part of the culture of the Graeco-Roman world, and they were entertaining stories. Folk like Hercules, born of the amours of Zeus with mortal women, were equally imaginary figures, one stage lower down; they were demigods, and if they reached the ranks of the Immortals it was due not so much to the accident of their birth as the achievement of their lives. As for the ruler cult, it was a convenient tool with which to bind together a religiously, culturally and politically disparate Empire. In the East men had for centuries been used to worshipping their rulers (without any thought that they embodied the essence of deity). When the Romans toppled the local potentates, they found it convenient to take over the worship that had been accorded to their defeated foes. Augustus had temples erected to him as *divus Augustus* in the East (whilst being more circumspect in the Roman West), but of course neither he nor anybody else imagined that by so doing he laid claim to embody the Godhead. Instead he prides himself in his *Res Gestae* (a chronicle of his virtuous actions) for his restoration of the temples and worship of the gods which had fallen on hard times during the preceding century of uncertainty and civil war. Frances Young is quite right in maintaining that, far from deriving the deity of Christ from the ruler cult, Christians asserted it as "a deliberate antithesis to the imperial cult". That is certainly part of the implication of Thomas' confession "My Lord and my God", and of the Samaritan woman calling Jesus "Saviour of the World" (John 4.42).

There has been a lot of talk in recent years about the *theios anēr*, the divine man, who was supposed to be a prototype in the ancient world for the divinity accorded to Jesus. When, however, you look for the evidence about these 'divine men', you find that it is all late. The one most commonly adduced, Apollonius of Tyana, was a rough contemporary of Jesus; but quite apart from the fact that his life and 'miracles' provide only the sketchiest of parallels for those of Jesus, we find that his biographer, Philostratus, lived at the end of the second century and wrote against a background where Christianity was a powerful and increasing force. What is more, as Frances Young points out, "*theios anēr* is by no means a fixed expression, and there is no such thing as a specific and defined class of people commonly called 'divine men'. The adjective *theios* by itself conveys little more than the sense 'inspired' " (p.100). Even if it did, we would have to reckon with two facts that make the *theios anēr* analogy hopelessly inept. The first is that belief in the deity of Jesus arose and maintained itself in a strongly monotheistic milieu, in striking contrast to polytheistic Graeco-Roman society. And secondly, the attenuated sense in which an Apollonius might be deemed *theios*, or an emperor might be called *divi filius* (son of a god—his predecessor) is utterly different from the way in which the early Christians used 'deity' of Jesus. As we have seen, they believed that "in Christ dwells all the fullness of the Godhead (the specific *theotēs*, not the loose *theiotēs*) bodily". And if we wonder how seriously we should take the 'deification' of the dying emperor we do not have far to look. Seneca poked fun at it in his *Pumpkinification of Claudius* in the fifties, and Vespasian, dying in the seventies, quipped "Alas, I fear I am becoming a god!" It is very difficult to see the Christian conviction about Jesus springing from such roots.

But no better ones have been put forward. Analogies from the Hermetic literature, the Gnostic Redeemer myth or the Mandaean literature are all post-Christian and therefore quite unable to account for the rise of Christian belief; they may all also be influenced (two of them certainly are) by Christian beliefs. Yet we find them churned out time and again by those who should know better. The plain fact is that there is no parallel whatever in the Graeco-Roman world to the exclusive claims to deity made for Jesus Christ. What is more, there could not be, because their religion was syncretistic and polytheist. How could it give birth to a faith in an incarnate Lord which was passionately monotheist and resisted syncretism to the extent of martyrdom? What is perfectly true is that, given their faith in the incarnate Lord, the early Christians used (sometimes rather unwisely) such partial parallels and analogies as they could find in the mythology of the pagans they were seeking to evangelise. That is simply good teaching method; to move from the known to the unknown, and to see foreshadowings of the truth even in the depraved legends of paganism.

Early in this century W. Bousset published an influential book, *Kyrios Christos* which argued that the attribution of Lordship to Jesus arose on pagan soil, where there were, as Paul acknowledged, 'lords many'. His 'deification' took shape, in other words, under Hellenistic influences as the Church spread.

To this there is a fatal objection. The title did not originate on pagan soil at all, but on Jewish. We have its original Aramaic in the formula *Maranatha* (1 Cor. 16.22). Depending on how you divide the word up, it means either 'Our Lord has come' or the invocation, 'O our Lord, come!'. It either attests Christ's incarnation or looks for his parousia. But it certainly addresses Jesus as *mara*, 'Lord'. The Old Testament was, of course, written in Hebrew not Aramaic (apart from a section of the Book of Daniel), but *mara* is a title for God in the Aramaic intertestamental documents that have come to light at Qumran (Aramaic *Enoch* 9.6; 89.31, 33 and 36 where the Greek has no *Kyrios*). The last plank of the supposed derivation of the deity of Jesus from pagan parallels has proved utterly untrustworthy.

Jewish parallels to the deity of Christ?

Perhaps we shall have better luck when we turn to Jewish sources. At first sight it is highly improbable that

Judaism should furnish any good parallels for the attribution of divine sonship to Jesus, because its creed was so unambiguously and jealously monotheistic. And the more one looks at it, the better grounded that first assumption seems to be.

The Jews had really learnt one lesson by the first century A.D. That is that there is only one God, and no runners up. They believed this so strongly that they would allow no images of the divine to decorate their synagogue walls (any image was bound to be an inadequate distortion). Tacitus in his *Histories* preserves the utter amazement of the Romans when Pompey burst his way into the Holy of Holies in the Temple at Jerusalem – and found no statuet here! So jealously did they stick to the Second Commandment that the Jews fought to the death rather than allow the Roman military standards, with their imperial medallions, to enter the Holy City. So seriously did Jews take their monotheism that they would not take the sacred name of God (Yahweh) upon their lips. At Qumran handbasins have been found in the scriptorium where the scrolls were written which were manifestly used for a ceremonial washing of the hands when the divine name was penned. In other words, if you had looked the whole world over for more stony and improbable soil in which to plan the idea of an incarnation you could not have done better than light upon Israel! Indeed, the Jews were unique. The Romans never could understand them, though they gave them a grudging kind of admiration. These people were different from all other races on earth; since they made no image of the deity they must be 'atheists', and such they called them. It was in this background, no other, that the conviction arose that God had incarnated himself in human flesh.

But surely Isaiah 7.14 indicates that they were at least sympathetic to the idea of a virgin birth? By no means. Virgin births did not figure in the religious concept of a Jew. He knew that the word translated 'virgin' in that

Isaiah passage, *almah*, meant merely 'young woman'. Marriage, not virginity was the Jewish ideal; so much so that they had no real word for a bachelor! And yet it was in this utterly unpropitious Jewish soil that the stories recorded in Matthew and Luke of the virgin birth of Jesus grew up, complete with their Jewish phraseology and Jewish genealogies. Incidentally, the stories owe nothing to parallels with pagan stories of intercourse between the gods and human women. The evidence has been exhaustively and decisively weighed in J. Gresham Machen's *The Virgin Birth of Christ*. If you are in doubt about it, read Machen's book. No, the birth stories, like the rest of the material which goes to make up the New Testament claim that in Jesus God was present in our world, are without analogy in pagan or Jewish literature.

To be sure, the king had long been called 'son of God' in an emasculated, adoptionist and figurative sense (Psalm 2.7). Ancient worthies such as Enoch invited speculation about their ascension to God – for did not the text of Holy Writ say, enigmatically, "And Enoch walked with God and he was not, for God took him"? Philosophers like Philo in Alexandria might seek to commend Judaism to a Hellenistic culture by speaking of the Law as personified Wisdom or pre-cosmic Reason (the Logos), but all of this is poles apart from the explicit, unambiguous claim of the many writers who go to make up the New Testament that Jesus was metaphysically not metaphorically one with God Almighty.

Why on earth, then, did these early Christians believe it, if there was no adequate parallel in either their Jewish background or Hellenistic paganism? It is not difficult to hazard a confident guess. They were persuaded by what they saw, heard and encountered of Jesus of Nazareth. He simply could not be confined to the category of the human. Reluctant, desperately reluctant as these Jewish monotheists were to accept the fact, Jesus must be more than man. Such seems to have been their trembling speculation after living with him for two or three years. It was rendered unshakable by the resurrection. Thereafter it became the conviction of the whole Christian Church, over against the alternatives of ebionism which denied the deity of Jesus, and docetism which denied his humanity. Difficult, almost impossible as it was to conceive of and assert, Christians held to the fact that Jesus was really human, and at the same time brought to us in his own person the presence and nature of God. A variety of reasons led them to this assurance.

His teaching

Their suspicions that there must be something different about Jesus were, I believe, first aroused by his teaching. "They were astonished at his teaching, for he taught them as one who had authority and not as the scribes" (Mark 1.22). It was the function of the scribes to teach and apply the Torah, the acknowledged revelation of God. But here was a man who had his own independent formula which denoted authority: "Amen, Amen I say unto you." It was unique. It meant that he set his teaching alongside that of the divinely inspired Old Testament. That Jesus accepted the divine authorship of the Old Testament is certain. He regarded it as God's inspired message (Mark 12.36, Matt. 22.31, John 5.37–47). As such it was absolutely authoritative (Matt. 26.53f, Luke 18.31, 22.37, Mark 12.24, John 10.34). Every strand in the New Testament evidence tells the same story. Jesus had the highest possible regard for the Scriptures, but was quite clear that his own teaching was no less authoritative: "Heaven and earth shall pass away, but my words shall not pass away." For authority, clarity, insight, profundity and power there is no parallel in the great religions which comes anywhere near the teachings of Jesus. "Never man spoke like this man" said the soldiers sent to arrest him. They were right. No ethical insight has emerged in the two thousand years since his day which cannot be derived from the teaching of the man of Nazareth. No higher conception of God has appeared. No more profound understanding of man. No error has been found in his teaching. It is peerless stuff, quite literally incomparable.

Where did it come from? He had not gone to the theological colleges of the day. He had not had much of an education. How is it, that unlike the teachings of Mao or Mohammed, his words apply to all men in every culture the world over? How is it that no improvements on his teachings have arisen? What was there in the heredity and environment of this first century Jewish carpenter to account for teaching such as the world has never been able to parallel? The most probable answer is the one he is reputed to have given: "My teaching is not mine, but his who sent me" (John 7.16).

His life

It is one thing to give the most profound and marvellous teaching on the ideals of living. It is quite another to live that way yourself. But all the evidence suggests that he did. There is not a shred of material anywhere in the New Testament to suggest that Jesus ever did a single thing which fell below the highest standards. In St. John's Gospel he claims "I do always those things which please him", referring to his Heavenly Father (8.29). And it would seem that he did. To be sure, it is impossible to prove that he never had an unkind thought or cherished an unworthy ambition. But let those who think so produce some hint of probability for their claim. All that has survived of Jesus points in precisely the opposite direction: to a person whose style of life fulfilled the highest ideals and whose teaching embodied them. A person who convinced friends and enemies alike that he had done nothing that was wrong. A person who not only taught love for the outcast and needy but practised it. A person who did not merely encourage men to bless their enemies but cried "Father forgive them" while they nailed him to the cross.

A person who, despite the most searching teaching he gave against hypocrisy, and man's accountability for wrong thoughts, no less than wrong actions (Matt. 5.21–30) never needs to apologise to anybody and never needs to confess failure before God. No wonder his disciples were convinced that in Jesus they had discovered "the true Light who gives light to every man" and that in him they had glimpsed perfection.

His claims

Jesus' personal self-consciousness has been the subject of intense scrutiny and debate in recent years. How much has been read back into the life of Jesus and placed on his lips by the early disciples? How much did he actually claim for himself?

Whether or not he claimed to be the 'Messiah', though interminably discussed, is almost beside the point. The title was inadequate and possessed political implications which had nothing to do with Jesus' mission. The Gospels indicate that he made little if any use of the term. When it was applied to him by others, such as Peter at Caesarea Philippi or his accusers at his trial, he preferred to interpret it in terms of the Servant of Yahweh, suffering for the sins of the world (Mark 8.29ff), or the glorious Son of Man who would return to judge the world (Mark 14.62). For what it is worth, though, it is hard to suppose that anyone would imagine him the Messiah after his shameful death on the cross unless he had indicated in some way that he was such while on earth. And it is equally hard to suppose that he would have been executed with 'The Jewish Messiah' as superscription over his cross (Mark 15.26), had there been no hint of it in his speech and behaviour. However that may be, the force of Jesus' claims does not lie in Messiahship. It does not even lie in titles like 'Son of Man', and 'the Son', which there is compelling evidence to suppose that he used of himself, and which certainly carried overtones which were more than human. No, the force lies in claims such as the following.

First, there is his explicit claim to forgive sins. This is an element in the tradition that is extremely well attested. "Your sins are forgiven you," said Jesus to a paralysed man on one occasion, and demonstrated the fact by healing him (Mark 2.1ff). No wonder the bystanders marvelled: "Who is this that forgives sins?" they asked. "Who can forgive sins but God alone?" Perhaps they were beginning to get the message.

A second claim involves worship. Now worship is properly offered to God alone, and the better a man is the more clearly he recognises this and acknowledges his own finitude and frailty. But not so with Jesus. Though amazingly humble and self-effacing in his personal life, his claims are very different. Research has shown that nobody in the history of Judaism ever addressed God with the intimate family word *Abba*, 'Daddy'. Yet Jesus did. Quite naturally, then, he accepts worship from his disciples. For him, the unique Son of the Father, it is no blasphemy. Thus when Peter falls at his feet in adoration after a fishing expedition and says, "Depart from me, for I am a sinful man, master" (Luke 5.8), Jesus does nothing to stop him. When Thomas falls at his feet after the resurrection and exclaims "My Lord and my God", Jesus does not rebuke him (John 20.28). No merely good man or great teacher would behave like that. Paul did not act in that way when the pagans of Lystra hailed him as a god—he recoiled in horror at the suggestion (Acts 14.4ff). Jesus, however, seems to have accepted worship as his due.

Perhaps the most decisive function which belongs to God is that of judgment. Yet here again Jesus seems quietly but firmly to have claimed this as his right. "The Father has committed all judgment to the Son" is how the Fourth Gospel puts it (5.22). In the famous parable of the sheep and the goats it is Jesus, the heavenly Son of Man who sits in judgment (Matt. 25.31)—and there are few critics indeed who would doubt the authenticity of this parable, displaying, as it does, an apparent doctrine of justification by works so markedly different from the teaching of St. Paul and the early Church. In Luke's account of the Last Supper we find Jesus looking forward to the kingdom he would inherit and the role of judgment he would exercise, along with those his faithful followers who had shared his role as the servant (Luke 22.27–30). In the Sermon on the Mount we find Jesus solemnly assuring his hearers that their eternal destiny depended not only on hearing but on building their lives upon his teaching. The crucial question at the Judgment Day will centre on their relationship to him (Matt. 7.23–27).

C. S. Lewis crisply expresses the point which must gradually have been dawning upon the minds of Jesus' disciples. In *Miracles* (p.32) he writes, "The discrepancy between the depth and sanity, and (let me add) shrewdness of his moral teaching and the rampant megalomania which must lie behind his theological teaching unless he is indeed God has never been satisfactorily got over." Nor has it.

His miracles

This is an exceedingly well attested, indeed, a universal aspect of the earliest tradition about Jesus. It is found throughout the four Gospels, Acts and in the Epistles. It is claimed extensively in the Apologists of the second century and is admitted in the later Jewish writings (though they maintain, as did the Pharisees in the lifetime of Jesus, that he did his miraculous acts through the power of the devil—an answer Jesus had no difficulty in demolishing, Mark 3.22ff). It remains, however, an area about which many modern theologians are exceedingly coy. This is because they do not believe miracles could happen. But if there is a personal Creator God, and if he did come to share our condition, who are we to lay down conditions of what might and might not be possible and fitting for him? The scientific thing to do is to examine the evidence. And the evidence in this case is overwhelming. There is no part of the New Testament that is not shot through and through with the conviction that the mighty works of Jesus disclosed the personal agency of God. A century of liberal *Lives* of Jesus, with their attempts to shrink him to our size and exclude the miraculous, are agreed on all sides to have failed. The records claim emphatically that Jesus healed the sick, cleansed the lepers, exorcised demonic forces that were gripping human lives, fed a multitude from a few loaves and walked on water, and on several occasions restored for a span of further life people who had very recently died (e.g. Mark 5.35–43, Luke 7.11–17, John 11.38–44). These were no conjuring tricks, no self-advertisement. They were the long awaited indications that God's great day of salvation had dawned, that the majesty and glory of Yahweh were present (see Isaiah 35.2–6, 61.1–4). The Jews could not deny these mighty works. The Romans were sufficiently well aware of them to back the mounting of a guard on his tomb, if we may believe Matthew's Gospel (27.62–66, 28.11–15).* And the evidence goes to show that many of the disciples came to believe in Jesus through the miracles. We read that his turning of water into wine at Cana "led many of his disciples to believe in him" (John 2.11). His raising of Lazarus had the same effect; "Many of the Jews who had come to visit Mary and had seen what Jesus did, put their faith in him" (John 11.45). His healing of the paralytic led the bystanders to glorify God saying, "We never saw anything like this" (Mark 2.12). His walking on the water and stilling the storm filled the disciples "with awe, and they said to one another 'Who is this, that even the wind and sea obey him?' " (Mark. 4.41).

* And I believe we may. To suppose that this is a piece of Christian apologetic completely fails to perceive the logic of the situation. See my *Man Alive*, p.40.

His fulfilment of Scripture

The first followers of Jesus, being Jews, had the highest regard for the Old Testament. It enshrined the oracles of God. Yet it was manifestly incomplete. For the Old Testament spoke of a day when God would judge the earth. It spoke of a king of David's stock whose dominion would be boundless. It spoke of all the families of mankind being blessed in Abraham. It spoke of one like a Son of Man coming to the Ancient of Days and receiving a kingdom that would never be destroyed, together with power, great glory and judgment. It spoke of a prophet like Moses arising among the people whose teaching would be unparalleled. It spoke of a Servant of the Lord whose death would atone for the sins of the people. It spoke of one who would forge a New Covenant between God and man, one who would put the Spirit of Yahweh into the hearts of men so that they could know God personally and have their sins wiped out. It spoke of God's kingly rule which he would establish on earth. It spoke of a stone, despised by the builders, which would become the keystone of the arch. It spoke of a priest like the legendary Melchizedek whom the Almighty would acclaim as Lord and welcome to his throne. The coming deliverer would fulfil the role of prophet, priest and king for ever. He would be born of David's line, but of a humble, despised family. His birthplace would be Bethlehem. He would both restore the fallen of Israel and be a light to lighten the Gentiles. He would be despised and rejected by the very people he came to rescue from their selfishness. He would die among wicked men and his tomb would be supplied by a rich man. But that would not be the end of him. He would live again, and the Lord's programme would prosper in his hands.

All of this came true with Jesus. Not some of it, all of it. There is no example in the literature of the world where the prophecies made centuries beforehand in a holy book were fulfilled in a historical person in this way. It amazed his followers, but it convinced them. They came to see him, the carpenter from Nazareth, the fulfilment of these ancient prophecies. He was born in Bethlehem of David's stock, and in a humble family. His teaching showed him to be the prophet like Moses. He was the suffering Servant of the Lord whose death could make men accepted with God, just as Abraham had been accepted irrespective of his merits. He was the one who had restored the fortunes of Israel and opened up the way of faith to the Gentiles. He had established the New Covenant between God and man, sealing it with his blood. He had made the ultimate sacrifice through his death, and no priesthood other than his would ever be needed again—for he had once and for all "given his life a ransom for many". His kingly rule would last for ever; veiled now, it would be apparent when he came to judge. His Spirit was already at work in the lives of the disciples, transforming them into his likeness.

It is more than probable that the disciples gained much of this insight with the benefit of hindsight, looking back on the life of Jesus in the light of the resurrection. The argument from prophecy, which made such notable converts during many centuries of the Church's life, is now often dismissed with contempt, as *vaticinia ex eventu*, prophecies after the event. However, even if all the prophecies could be described in this way, the situation would be without parallel. Nowhere in literature do we find all the lines of historical perspective in prophecy converging on a single individual. Nowhere else do we find men claiming that every hint of future deliverance delivered by holy men over a period of a thousand years has come true in a person of their acquaintance.

But it is not possible to dismiss all the prophecies as the products of hindsight. The most impressive prophecies which Jesus is said to have fulfilled concern the circumstances of his birth and of his death, the two areas of a person's existence which it is hardest for him to organise!

What is more, the distinctive new way of interpreting Scripture which we find throughout the New Testament shows every sign of being initiated by a particularly powerful and original mind. The New Testament writers, as C. H. Dodd observed at the end of his magisterial study *According to the Scriptures*, bear clear testimony to the identity of that powerful and original mind: it belonged to Jesus. Are we compelled to reject their testimony? Or is there not strong reason to suppose that this amazing figure, Jesus, did fulfil the varied hopes of the Scriptures, that he knew and taught his disciples that he was doing just that, and that their discovery "in all the Scriptures of things concerning himself" goes back to Jesus himself?

All of these straws in the wind were such as the disciples could, in principle, have grasped during the lifetime of Jesus. But the New Testament is very honest. It does not attempt to spare the twelve. It does not hide their doubts and blindness and failure to understand. Why should it? The inconceivable was taking place. The Lord was visiting his people. No wonder they were slow to understand.

What finally convinced them was the cross and resurrection.

His cross and resurrection

It is impossible to exaggerate the importance of the death of Jesus in the eyes of his disciples. In a biography you find only a few pages referring to the death of the person concerned. In a news bulletin the announcement of a man's death is followed immediately by some highlights of his life. Not so with Jesus. The Gospels are no mere biographies. They belong to an entirely different genre, expressing good news. And the good news centres on the death of Jesus. The Christians glory in it. The cross, which you might have thought would crush such faith as they had, in fact lit it into a mighty blaze. And that is a very remarkable thing. Remarkable to start believing in your leader once he is dead and gone. Remarkable to start believing that he is God's anointed rescuer once he has signally failed to produce any solution of the Roman problem, and has instead been executed by them as a pretender to power—who failed. Most remarkable of all when you recall that the Old Testament pronounced God's curse on the man who hung exposed on a cross. Remarkable, but true. The Christian movement only began to catch light once Jesus was crucified.

Somehow in that cross his puzzled disciples saw into the very heart of God. They saw that "God was in Christ, reconciling the world to himself" (2 Cor. 5.19). They saw that if he bore a curse, the curse was ours (Gal. 3.13); that if he staggered and fell on his way to crucifixion it was under the weight of our sins which he carried to the cross (1 Pet. 2.24). They appreciated that, in the words of that earliest creed of the thirties, "Christ died for our sins according to the Scriptures" (1 Cor. 15.3). Mark has his own graphic way of expressing the meaning of the cross as he saw it. After recounting the death of Jesus he immediately continues, "And the veil of the temple was ripped in half from top to bottom." That curtain was placed there to keep people out of the most sacred Holy of Holies in the temple, the place where God's presence was located. But when Jesus died, the curtain that kept men from God was torn apart; the way into his presence was made available to all. And Mark symbolically and significantly tells us that the centurion in charge of the execution makes the distinctively Christian confession, "This man was the Son of God"—himself the prototype of the thousands of Gentiles who had been brought into God's presence through Christ crucified by the time that Mark wrote his Gospel (15.38ff). In the death of Jesus on the cross the disciples saw through to the very heart of God, the depth of his love for sinful men, the extent to which he was willing to go in order to rescue us from the results of our self-will. Paradoxically, that cross which should have been the nadir of their hopes was in fact the birthplace of their assurance that in dealing with Jesus they were dealing with God.

But was their interpretation of his death correct? It would have been impossible to say, had there been no resurrection. How could they have been sure that "he was put to death for our offences" if it were not that he was "raised for our justification"? (Rom. 4.25). The Gospels abound in indications given by Jesus that after his death he would be vindicated by the resurrection (Mark 2.20, 8.31, 9.31, 10.34, 12.10ff, Matt. 12.40ff). Let us assume that they are all prophecies after the event: at least the fact of the resurrection vindicated Jesus' position as Lord and Christ (Acts 2.34–6). It showed that he was defined as Son of God (Rom. 1.4). The resurrection pulsates throughout the New Testament as God's decisive act, vindicating his Son Jesus. It was this mighty act of God which confirmed their Christology.

But Professor Hick would have us suppose that the resurrection would not have necessarily confirmed Jesus' deity in the eyes of his followers. He argues (*op. cit.* p.170ff) that plenty of people seem to have been raised from the dead without anybody supposing that they were divine: Jairus' daughter, Lazarus, and the widow of Nain's son, to mention but a few. Why should it be any different with Jesus? As Bishop Neill has shown elsewhere in this volume, Hick has made a gross and elementary category confusion. The disciples did not think that Jesus had a short extension of this present life: Lazarus and Jairus' daughter were restored to this life and in due course had to suffer death. They believed that Jesus had been raised to a new quality of life: no mere extension of the old earthly life – he was raised to share the undying life of God. "Christ being raised from the dead, dies no more," they maintained (Rom. 6.9). As St. John expresses it in his vision of Christ, "Fear not, I am the first and the last, and the living one; I died and behold I am alive for evermore, and I have the keys of Death and Hades" (Rev. 1.17). This was no resuscitation, but resurrection. It was the breaking in, in one person, Jesus, of God's final destiny for all his people. In the resurrection of Jesus they saw anticipated the ultimate destiny of believers. They saw in the risen Christ "the first fruits of those who have fallen asleep". He is, thus far, the first and only such fruit: the rest of the crop will follow at the last day. "But each in his own order: Christ the firstfruits, then at his coming those who belong to Christ" (1 Cor. 15.20,23).

It is an astonishing fact that most of the writers in *The Myth of God Incarnate* have very little to say about the resurrection, which is, after all, the crux as to whether the Jesus story is myth or history. None of them have begun to come to terms with the evidence afforded by the New Testament itself, and expounded by men like Karl Barth and Wolfhart Pannenberg. Professor Wiles alludes very briefly to it and astonishingly describes the New Zealander, Lloyd Geering's book, *Resurrection—a Symbol of Hope* as "well argued" (p.160). Here is a sample of that book. Judge for yourself:

"Both the literary form and the actual content of the earliest version, viz. the Marcan, show not only that it definitely contains some legendary elements, but that it is unlikely to have had any historical foundation at all." He asserts that when this Gospel was written, 'it is likely that none of the original apostles was still living" so there was "no one to raise authoritative objections" (p.56f). It is hardly surprising that Geering's book is discounted by serious students of the resurrection.

The only other member of the symposium who addresses himself to the resurrection is Mr. Goulder. I have already summarised his conclusions on p.15 above. A conversion-vision experienced by Peter, the power of hysteria infusing the disciples with Easter faith—and we are on the way to carrying Jesus to divinity and his teachings to every corner of the globe (p.59). He advises us, on the basis of Occam's razor, to prefer a natural psychologising explanation for the 'appearances' to the traditional belief that God miraculously raised Jesus from the dead. He admits that his view looks indistinguishable from that of a humanist, but wants to safeguard some distinctiveness for Jesus by calling him "the man of universal destiny". By this he understands "Jesus to have been destined by God to establish the community of selfless love in the world". But could not Occam's razor be invoked to remove that unnecessary hypothesis, God? However that may be, the psychologising interpretation of the resurrection appearances has little enough to commend it. In the first place, as Ulrich Wilckens has acidly pointed out "It is quite impossible that disciples of Jesus should have reacted to the catastrophe of his death by the conviction suddenly dawning on them that he had been raised from the dead – which had never previously been asserted in Israel of any mortal" (*The Significance of the Message of the Resurrection for Faith in Jesus*, ed. C. F. D. Moule, p.61). There can be no question of wish-fulfilment about it. They neither wished nor expected anything of the sort. Their leader had been crucified like many another before him. In the natural course of events they would have scattered to their homes with shattered hopes, like all the other followers of messianic pretenders.

Second, as Bishop Robinson puts it, "If the appearances had been merely psychic phenomena, one would expect the sense that Jesus was alive to have grown progressively less vivid once the disciples ceased to be 'in touch', and those who had not seen the evidence to be as sceptical as third parties usually are to such supposed communications from the dead—let alone to reports of miraculously empty graves. But in fact the conviction became only the more settled once the appearances had ceased, and those who had not seen were won to just as living a faith as those who had." (*The Interpreter's Dictionary of the Bible*, Vol. 4, p.48.) He goes on to point out that the ground of appeal was not so much past appearances as present experience of the living Christ. This is what made and sustained the

Christian Church. "And the very existence of the Church not merely as the historical embodiment of past phenomena but as the embodiment of a present faith, is itself a major part of the evidence for the resurrection. Indeed, it was this present conviction, which thrills through the letters, that alone caused the other evidence to be preserved."

Third, a man like St. Paul knew quite a lot about visions. He experienced them (2 Cor. 12.2) and he was quite clear in his own mind that what he saw on the Damascus Road was no vision. As Professor Lampe put it, these early Christians "were absolutely convinced that there was an encounter, which they hadn't dreamed up for themselves, between the objective presence of Christ, 'outside' themselves, and their own selves. That happened". (*The Resurrection of Christ* p.18.)

In point of fact, hallucinations tend to affect a particular type of person: but the appearances of the risen Jesus came alike to a Mary Magdalene, a James, a Paul, a Thomas and a Peter! Hallucinations are generally associated with a particular place or time and recur over a long period. These appearances were restricted to forty days and took place at morning, noon, and night. They were experienced on seashore and roadside, in an upper room and in a garden—the locality made no difference.

Are we to suppose that this entire Christian movement, which demonstrably began in the thirties of the first century, and was differentiated from Judaism only by the conviction that the Messiah had come and had been raised by God to his right hand, arose from nothing more than a hallucination? Then indeed the myth would be stranger than history. If the Easter faith arose without any Easter fact to trigger it off we should indeed have cause for amazement. It is a very recent and ill-grounded development of criticism to argue that the empty tomb was no part of the earliest preaching. As Dodd insists, when the early Christians maintained "He rose from the dead", they "took it for granted that his body was no longer in the tomb. If the tomb had been visited it would have been found empty. The Gospels supplemented this by saying that it *was* visited and it *was* found empty." (*The Founder of Christianity* p.166.) To be sure Paul does not explicitly mention the empty tomb in 1 Corinthians 15, though he alludes to it: what else could be meant by his quotation of that early creed on which he had been nourished, "that he died for our sins according to the Scriptures, that he was buried, and that he was raised on the third day in accordance with the Scriptures" (1 Cor. 15.4)? Why should he say more? He was not writing to convince the Corinthians of the resurrection; he was writing to remind them that he had convinced them on this matter years ago. The point which always annoys advocates of psychologising explanations of the resurrection, but remains unanswerable, is this. Why did nobody produce the body? That would have been the surest way to silence this troublesome new teaching about the resurrection of Jesus from the dead and nip the whole thing in the bud. Nobody did produce that evidence: nobody could.

All the Gospel accounts agree in their assertion that the tomb was empty on the first Easter Day. The focus of their interest is, of course, not in the abandoned chrysalis case but in the butterfly, so there is much more about the risen Christ than there is about his empty tomb. But that they believed his tomb was empty, and that they could not have believed he was alive had they known his tomb was still occupied, is evident. We have a good deal of evidence about beliefs in Pharisaic Judaism about the resurrection, and though, of course, they did not expect it until the Last Day, it was always envisaged as uncompromisingly physical. The disciples simply would not have understood the modern attempt to preserve some sort of resurrection for Jesus while his body lay mouldering in the tomb. That would not be resurrection, but imagination.

Their experience of the risen Christ, the fact of the

empty tomb, the appearances of the risen Lord, the inauguration of the Christian Church—all of this provides strong reason to suppose that Jesus did in fact rise from the dead. The changed lives of the disciples, changed aspirations, changed morals, new joy, peace and endurance —all of these things sprang from the conviction that death has been defeated by God in Christ. The remarkable thing is that millions of Christians the world over continue to bear witness to the same faith. Millions each year are converted to it from all religions and from none. It is the coping stone on the New Testament insistence that in Jesus God has uniquely, decisively and personally shown us what he is like; has dealt with our alienation by entering into it and bearing it on the cross; and has conquered the last and greatest enemy of man, death, by his glorious resurrection. Such and no less is the confident assurance of the New Testament writers.

CHAPTER TWO

Jesus and Myth

STEPHEN NEILL

I DID NOT KNOW quite what to expect of *The Myth of God Incarnate*. The last thing that I expected was that it would produce loud laughter. But this is what happened.

A venture in redaction-criticism

Michael Goulder opens Chapter 3 with a myth which he cites in the following form:

... the Pope being told by the cardinals that the remains of Jesus had been dug up in Palestine. There was no doubt that it was Jesus—all the Catholic archaeologists were agreed. "Oh", said the Pope, "what do we do now?" "Well," said the cardinals, "there is only one hope left; there is a Protestant theologian in America called Tillich—perhaps you could get him on the phone." So Tillich was telephoned, and the position was explained to him. There was a long pause at the end of which the voice said, "You mean to say he really existed?"

Now it is well known to all scholars that in all the oldest and best authorities the myth is given in the following form:

Such a grave and such a skeleton have indeed been

discovered in Palestine. A visitor to Rudolf Bultmann puts to him the question what effect this will have on his faith. After long thought Bultmann delivers himself of the judgment, "So he really did live then?"

It happens that I am able to supply the historical core which is found at the heart of this, as of most myths. When a television programme on the work and thought of Bultmann was being prepared, Vernon Sproxton visited the great man, and in the course of a long conversation put to him just this question: supposing that such a grave and such a skeleton were discovered, would this have any effect on his faith in Jesus Christ? Bultmann's only answer was to roar with laughter at the absurd suggestion that it could have any effect whatever.

Clearly this is a case for careful redaction-criticism. It is well known that the alterations in the myth made by a writer clearly reveal the trends and tendencies to which he has been subjected.

Why the introduction of the poor old Pope? I fear that this is a recrudescence of the old 'No Popery' cry so characteristic of the English people as recently as sixty years ago. At that time many Anglicans were prepared to find the Pope lurking under every bush; the place of the Pope has now been worthily taken over by Karl Marx.

Mr. Goulder is very anxious to be 'with it'. Hence the introduction of the telephone, when a letter would perfectly well have done.

And why in the world the wholly inappropriate Paul Tillich? I fear that this can only be explained as a Tillich fixation imposed upon Mr. Goulder in the nursery.

I find it more difficult to explain the omission of Bultmann. I have been tempted to think up a number of fantastic explanations; but, always preferring prose to poetry, I wonder whether the obvious explanation is the right one—that Mr. Goulder has never heard of Rudolf Bultmann? It is possible that the substitutions have been made in a pre-Goulder era; but this would make no difference to the argument; it would merely mean that we are dealing with a school, and not with the views of a single writer.

With this brilliant mythopoeic faculty, it is not surprising that Mr. Goulder has gone for illumination to the darkest corridor of biblical study, Samaritan speculation. Even his colleague Mrs. Young seems somewhat hesitant to go with him into the tulgy wood; but he may be assured that if he comes back from his adventure with a single slithy tove, we shall, as in Lewis Carroll's Jabberwock, chortle in our joy.

A marvellous demonstration of the difficult art of making bricks without clay!

Hellenistic mythology and the New Testament —contrasted

We are on firmer ground in the two contributions of Mrs. Young—on the Hellenistic background of New Testament thoughts, and on developments in the patristic period. In each chapter Mrs. Young has tried to do too much and to put into a chapter what would only be dealt with in a book. The result is compression, simplification and a number of questionable statements. But there is real material here, and it is clear that a number of pennies have dropped.

When I was working intensively in this field rather more than half a century ago, the Mandaeans were all over the place. They still sprawl on almost every page of even the latest edition of Bultmann's commentary on the Fourth Gospel. But by 1930 Cambridge had decided that "there ain't no gold in them there Mandaeans"—a point of view more elegantly expressed by C. H. Dodd, *The Interpretation of the Fourth Gospel* pp.115–130 (especially the summing up on p.130). It is good that in Mrs. Young's work the Mandaeans hardly appear.

At the same period the dying and rising god myth was a

very popular theme. I well remember my enchantment at reading in 1918, as a schoolboy, J. G. Frazer's *Adonis, Attis, Osiris*. There were dying and rising gods all over the place; clearly Jesus was a superb example of the myth of the dying and rising god. We now know that there is no example anywhere in this literature of the myth being applied to any known and identifiable historical figure. If the disciples did indeed use the myth for the elucidation of the doctrine of the resurrection of Jesus, they were not following any familiar pattern, but were embarking on a wildly original intellectual adventure. This is another penny that has dropped; there is less here than one might have expected about this touching and picturesque myth of the northern winter and spring.

A great deal has been made of the pre-Pauline Hellenistic Christian congregations, in which much of the fusion of Hellenistic ideas with the Christ-story is alleged to have taken place. We now know that such congregations did not exist; from the very beginning, the Greek translation of the Old Testament played a major part in forming the ideas of Christian believers. These Hellenistic congregations were invented by German scholars in the early years of this century; they are purely mythological, and are rightly so treated by Mrs. Young.

My only complaint about Mrs. Young is that she is still far too conservative and not yet fully emancipated from the Germans. She could have gone much further than she has.

We now know that it is impossible to use second-century evidence for the explanation of first-century material; the two centuries were so different that they have to be treated separately. This means that Mrs. Young's section on Apollonius of Tyana and all that could simply have been omitted as irrelevant.

We can now be almost certain that there never was a pre-Christian Gnostic redeemer; when a redeemer appears in Gnostic sources, this is almost certainly a borrowing from Christian doctrines rather than the other way about.

We now know that there is no example in the non-Christian literature of anything that can be treated as a parallel to the birth-narratives in the Gospels. The so-called parallels are for the most part either what Dale Moody has elegantly called "mythological fornication", or obvious compliments to a person regarded as specially eminent. There is nothing in the least like the sober and restrained dignity of the Gospels. It is clear that there is no trace whatever of Hellenistic influence in those purely Jewish narratives; parallels to them are to be sought in the Old Testament and nowhere else; and they may well represent the convictions and experiences of those commonly called the "quiet in the land".

Mrs. Young quotes (without reference) A. D. Nock as having said that "the Christian hope has its roots in Palestine; Christian theology and above all Christology have theirs in Alexandria". I must ask leave to disagree with my old Cambridge friend and rival. I pleaded with him earnestly to write the comprehensive book on Hellenistic religion which he alone could have written. But, alas, that book which we so sorely need was never written. Nock knew a great deal about the Hellenistic world. But he knew not a word of Hebrew (or perhaps two or three), and he was not very well at home in the Bible. He told me that when he was asked to write a book about St. Paul, he knew nothing about the subject and had to learn as he went along; this, I think gives its freshness to what I regard as being still the best introduction to the thought of St. Paul in any language. I would rewrite his sentence as follows: "Christian hope and theology have their roots in Palestine; Alexandrian theology and above all Christology have theirs in Alexandria." This I believe to be true. I think Mrs. Young should have quoted the judgment of W. K. C. Guthrie, who, after enumerating eleven senses in which the word *logos* is used in Greek, gives it as his judgment that none of these usages bears any relation to the logos-doctrine of the Fourth Gospel (*History of Greek Philosophy*, Vol. I, pp. 420–24).

When I was working specially on the term *Sōtēr*, 'Saviour', I put to myself frequently the question, Where is there any *ethical* connotation in the word outside biblical sources? Where can I find a parallel to "he shall save his people from their sins" (Matt. 1.21)? I thought that I had found the answer in the close collocation of salvation with righteousness in the Second Isaiah (Sanday and Headlam misled me here); but closer acquaintance with Semitic usage revealed that in these contexts 'salvation' means 'deliverance from captivity' and 'righteousness' refers in the main to the vindication of God's honour, impugned among the Gentiles through the captivity of his people. The ethical note is faint if it is there at all. I have never found any parallel, in either Hellenistic or Jewish sources, to the New Testament concept of salvation. This is another example of the splendid independence and creativity of early Christian thinking. As I have said, I wish that Mrs. Young had gone further than she has. But the impressive mass of materials that she has assembled does strongly confirm what I have just stated. Of course there are certain parallels. The apostles wrote in Greek. If you write in Greek, you must use Greek words; every Greek word has a long history, and multiple associations, some of which may be superficially related to New Testament concepts. Many of these parallels hardly so much as illustrate the New Testament; it is quite inconceivable that they could have been the source of New Testament thinking. We must be grateful to Mrs. Young for making this as clear as she has. I have a feeling that she is really a Nicene lamb strayed from the fold, and that she will never be really happy until she has found her way back. And I wish that before writing her chapters she had been able to see C.F.D. Moule's *Origin of Christology*, which has come to my hands just in time to be used in the preparation of this chapter. If it had been available a little earlier, I wonder whether the book under consideration could have been written in anything like its present form.

Dubious analogies

I am less happy with other sections of the book, especially with those that deal directly with the question of myth; indeed I am not sure whether the writers have reached a clear understanding and a consistent use of this term, the very nature of which is as quicksilver.

Professor Wiles tells us that he is prepared to accept the creation myth, if it is understood as a statement of the fact that the universe is dependent on a transcendent, creative source (p.159). Well and good. But it must be borne in mind that his Hindu and Buddhist friends will be laughing in their sleeves at his credulity. We know that nothing exists; why then should we bother with a myth to explain to us the existence of that which we know to be non-existent? Of the myth of the fall, that sublime analysis of the human situation, he is prepared to write that "I believe it is true that men fall below the highest that they see and that they could achieve" (p.160). Only a very good man could write like that about the human situation. What would the writers of this book say if someone came to them and asked, "Sir, what shall I do to be saved?" I have a slight feeling that the answer might be, "Enrol for my course of lectures on Christian doctrine (or, better still, comparative religion); the lectures start on Monday."

I am even less happy about the illustrations Professor Wiles gives of the changes that have taken place in the expression of Christian doctrine.

It is true that at the Reformation the mediaeval doctrine of transubstantiation, together with the philosophy of substance and accidents on which it was based, was given up by large sections of the Christian Church. But in my extreme evangelical days I was taught devoutly to believe in the real presence of Christ in the Eucharist; not of course in any kind of localised presence such as St. Thomas Aquinas had repudiated, still less in a miraculous conversion of the elements into something else. It is clear that essentially the same thing was being said in a different and more acceptable way. But, if I came to believe that the Eucharist is not a joyful meeting with a living Lord but a rather pathetic meditation on a friend long since dead, I would become a Quaker tomorrow. But I would not cease to be a Christian.

Professor Wiles' second illustration is from the abandonment of the doctrine of verbal inspiration. This was indeed a crisis. Dr. W. R. Maltby once remarked that the suffering caused by the process of transition from one view to another probably exceeded that caused by several world wars. I lived through this crisis myself. But those of us who had the good fortune to be taught the Old Testament by the undeservedly forgotten Alexander Nairne found, after three or four weeks, that our feet were once again upon the rock; not precisely the same rock, but not a logan stone.

With the principle of the incarnation the case is entirely different. "When the brains were out the man would die." This is not a case of saying the same thing in a different way, but of saying something entirely different in an entirely different way. I have said many times in speech and writing that, if it could be proved conclusively that Jesus of Nazareth never existed, I would still regard the four Gospels as the best news ever given to mankind. These little books show us, as no other writing of any other religion has shown us, how men ought to live, and how human life can be made dignified, even noble—in point of fact, human. But to suggest that such a faith would have more than a superficial resemblance to the faith by which I try to live today, would simply be to use words without any reference to meaning.

Professor Wiles asks whether old-fashioned Unitarianism is the only alternative to the Nicene faith. If the

T–C

question is put in this way, the answer is certainly No; there are many possible alternatives. But if the question is asked in relation to the book *The Myth of God Incarnate*, the answer is that what is being offered to us is almost precisely the old Unitarianism which has had a distinguished history over many generations.

The Girton Conference, and The Myth of God Incarnate

The writers correctly state in the preface that "there is nothing new in the main theme of this book and we make no pretence to originality". In consequence many older readers will have again and again the sense of *déjà vu*. I am old enough to remember vividly the Girton Conference of the Modern Churchmen's Union held in 1921. There is a rather unsympathetic but not inaccurate account of this conference and of what flowed from it in Roger Lloyd, *The Church of England, 1900–1965*, pp. 263–278. The conference caused a considerable stir—we were less used in those days than we are now to the eccentricities of Anglican clerics. But the questions dealt with were much the same as those handled in the volume we are now studying; many of the arguments are the same. The vocabulary has changed, and of course we live in a different world. The feeling remains that I have heard all this before. Some of those who read the report of the conference, wooed by the mellifluous tones of Dr. H. D. A. Major and his friends, found that they had abandoned the Nicene faith, as the writers of this work have abandoned it. Professor Wiles was at one time a conservative evangelical, and loyally affirms his debt to those who guided him in those days; but those days have long since passed away. Mr. Goulder admits to having been at one time a Chalcedonian (p.49). Apparently he was knocked off his perch as easily as the curate in *The Way of All Flesh* was knocked off his by the unbelieving tailor. At the time the Modern Churchmen believed themselves to be in the van of adventurous progress in Christian thinking;

they did not know that they were attending the funeral of the old liberalism.

The reaction had already set in. By 1921 Edwyn Clement Hoskyns was back in Cambridge, and before long had gathered round him a group of ardent disciples. He was my friend, but never my teacher. Hoskyns came nearer than any other English theologian in this century to creating a school after the German model. Before long the more strident voice of Karl Barth began to speak through Hoskyns and became widely heard in the English-speaking world. Even after fifty years the influence still continues, and the voice of Hoskyns is heard speaking through Michael Ramsey.

The stream of those passing from a Nicene to a non-Nicene or even an anti-Nicene position was not very large, but was not without its influence all through the period between the wars. Much more interesting as a theological phenomenon—the most interesting, I think, in the world of the twentieth century—was the stream of these moving in the opposite direction. Perhaps the most outstanding was that wise and beloved ecumenist Nathaniel Micklem. When Micklem wrote *The Galilean* he was a liberal perhaps rather to the left of T. R. Glover and other liberal teachers of that day. In middle life he grew to a definite Nicene faith, robust, balanced and beautifully expressed. No one ever doubted either his intelligence or his integrity. William Temple falls almost but not quite into the same category; an interesting anthology could be made of the various things that he said about Chalcedon in the course of his teaching ministry. John Baillie, best and most eloquent of theological popularisers in the best sense of the term, wrote a book called *The Place of Jesus Christ in Modern Christianity,* in which he put forward very much the views expressed in the work which we are studying. Then he also underwent some kind of a Nicene conversion; although I knew him well I never enquired into the circumstances. But I did once refer in his presence to the book just mentioned; he was obviously embarrassed, and said, "I don't quite remember what I said in that book." He preferred even to forget the work by which he made his name, a highly intelligent book entitled *The Interpretation of Religion*. On the Roman Catholic side I will mention only two who have found it possible to accept the full Roman Catholic faith, the French existentialist philosopher Gabriel Marcel, and the distinguished mathematician Sir Edward Appleton. If it comes to counting up brain-power, the favourable balance is on the side of the Nicenes.

Husks—or bread?

I wish that I were more certain as to what exactly is being offered us in exchange for the Nicene faith. It seems that we are being offered a God who loved us a little, but not enough to wish to become one of us; a Jesus who did not rise from the dead, and therefore offers no answer to the great and bitter problems of humanity; and a gospel which is just one of many forms of salvation, and perhaps not that which is most suitable to modern Western man. If this is so, we may perhaps be excused if we say respectfully to our friends that it looks to us remarkably like the diet which the younger son enjoyed in the far country. However, if that is the food they appreciate, and if they find it to be nutritive, far be it from us to deny them a single husk; but it would not be honest to pretend that it bears much resemblance to what we so liberally enjoy in the Father's house. We might even be tempted to whisper in their ear that the door to the Father's house is always open, and that there is a specially warm welcome for returning Pelagians.

The writers tell us that they have met five times for discussion during the past three years. I wish that they had met ten times over six years, and delayed till then the publication of their book. We should then, I think, have had a better book. One of the writers, dealing with the question of resurrection, gives us a long list of occurrences of resurrection mentioned in Scripture (pp.170–1), and does not mention the obvious fact that not one of these occurrences bears the smallest resemblance to the resurrection of Jesus. Those were all instances of suspended mortality; all those people were one day going to die. The New Testament writers did not say of Jesus that he rose from the dead, but that "Christ being raised from the dead dieth no more; death hath no more dominion over him" (Rom. 6.9), and that, because in him death has been vanquished, the new creation is already here (2 Cor. 5.17). If this passage in *The Myth of God Incarnate* had been shown up to me in an essay by a first-year theological student, I would have put my pen through the paragraph, marked the essay gamma, and told the student to do the work all over again. This is not to say that what the New Testament asserts is necessarily true; still less that it necessarily follows that the believers concluded that Jesus was divine because he was raised from the dead. The same writer, on p.173, uses the term "deification". This gives the whole case away. I would be inclined to agree that the disciples came to understand the divine nature of their Lord through constant fellowship with him rather than simply through the events of the resurrection. I would also fully agree that the story in which we believe is wholly a story about God; the fundamental error in the study of Christology is the assumption that it is a doctrine about Jesus Christ, when it is, of course, a doctrine about God. All I am pleading for is that, if the New Testament is referred to, it should be allowed to speak for itself, and that we should be allowed to hear what it really does say. I am sure that, with rather more careful editing, this and other weaknesses would have been removed.

As in the volume of Girton 1921, there is much in this volume that is agreeable. There is a pleasing freedom of spirit (not unmixed with occasional levity), a determination that no question, however difficult, shall remain unasked, a confidence in the power of truth to shine by its own light, an unmistakable devotion to the Lord whom we all seek. For all these things we may be most thankful. It remains the fact that other Christians have been pondering all these problems for many years, with almost all the evidence here set forth available to them, I hope with equal openness of mind and a readiness, in Platonic phrase, to follow the argument whithersoever it may lead, and yet have reached conclusions very different from those set forth here. And naturally we think that our conclusions are better than their conclusions. But this means that for the time being we are scattered vessels of his fleet. Yet we can salute one another in passing. We can trust that, as our colleagues set forth again on their adventure brave and new, they may find treasures of truth such as now are hidden from them, as doubtless also from us. And we can hope that, in the infinite mercy and goodness of God, we may all in the end safe within the harbour meet.

CHAPTER THREE

Jesus and History

STEPHEN NEILL

HE WHO SAYS 'Jesus' says also 'history'. The early Christians recognised this, and by putting Pontius Pilate into their creeds, transformed the second-rate governor of a second-rate Roman sub-province into the second-best known man in the whole of human history. It is often said that the writers of the New Testament were not interested in history, and that Paul in particular does not go back to the story of a life lived in Galilee and Judaea. Such statements go contrary to a great deal of the evidence. Paul is inconsistent in his use of names and titles for Jesus of Nazareth, and the manuscripts have further confused the evidence of their diversity. But when Paul uses the simple Jewish name 'Jesus', as he does five times in 2 Corinthians 4.7–15, he is consciously turning back precisely to that earthly life and to the historic events from which the Christian faith cannot be separated.

In the past few years Professor G. A. Wells has written two volumes to show, as did Arthur Drews before him, that Jesus of Nazareth never really existed but is the creation of the minds of the early Christians. The first volume, *The Jesus of the Early Christians*, was commended by Professor Hugh Trevor-Roper, who ought to know better. Of the second, Bishop John Robinson, who would not be classed as an arch-conservative, has written a review which is a masterpiece of the art of delicate dissection and of courteous annihilation. There is no heresy so dead that someone will not attempt to resuscitate it; there is no error so frequently denounced that someone will not try once more to deck it in the garments of truth. With some critical reservations it can safely be asserted that Jesus belongs to the world of history.

The meaning of 'history'

This means that, if we are to consider Jesus seriously, we must have some idea of what the word 'history' means; and this is not so easily arrived at as might be thought. Though it is in one sense contingent, in another sense history is as absolute as anything could possibly be.

History deals with the unique, the unpredictable, the unrepeatable, the unalterable and the irreversible. Some slight elucidation of each word may be in place:

Unique. No historic situation is really like any other. We may detect certain resemblances; this is not the only time in history that I have sat down in front of my typewriter to compose an article. But, on careful observation, it is invariably found that the differentials are far more numerous than the similarities and that the assumption of similarity can be a dangerous guide.

Unpredictable. The similarities do make it possible for us to do some intelligent guessing about the future. Long ago I foresaw that the Russian Revolution, like the French, was likely to issue in a military dictatorship; but I did not foresee the full horrors of the Stalin regime. I know India well, but I did not imagine that Mrs. Gandhi could so easily be toppled from power. I do not think that anyone foresaw that Mr. Lynch would come back to power with the largest majority in the history of the Irish republic.

Unrepeatable. Once the past has become the past, it is impossible ever to get it back, or to reproduce exactly the situation and the cause that produced it. We may look back with regret or nostalgia; we may reconstruct the past in imagination. But we can never get back there; we can never bring about just that collocation of circumstances that led to the event, whatever it may have been.

Unalterable. As my hand hovers over the typewriter, I have before me all the resources of the English dictionary. Once my fingers have descended, all the other possibilities are excluded. I can of course cross the word out and start again; but that does not alter the fact that I typed just that and nothing else. And not even God can cause me not to have typed that word. He could make me tear up the sheet, or lose it. He could see to it that this article is never printed, and that no one else ever knows what I wrote. This does not alter the fact that I wrote it, and that fact not even God can alter.

Irreversible. Here history differs radically from both philosophy and science. A logical argument can be worked in either direction. I may pour sulphuric acid on copper and produce copper sulphate; but I may equally well take copper sulphate and by electrolysis bring it back to the separate states of copper and sulphuric acid with very little loss. With history this cannot be done; it flows only in one direction. (In our historical studies, we may trace the story backwards; but this is something quite different.) Adam, after his experience of an inhospitable world, may have wished to re-enter Eden; but the cherub with the flaming sword was in the way. Israel in the wilderness often wanted to go back to Egypt; but the word of the Lord came with the most strenuous prohibition—the way could only be forward. So it is that, whether we like it or not, time carries us forward through the years in only one direction: there is no turning back.

This linear character of history, as a story which had a beginning, is in movement, and will have a climax, or at least an end, seems to have been a discovery of the Jews. Five centuries before Herodotus the father of history began to write, unnamed historians at the court of David and Solomon were writing memorable history in terms of a divine purpose for mankind. Greek and Roman history tends to be circular; the thought of the everlasting return is never far away. And so it was in much of the religion of the Levant in the days of the early Christians: "Cease, Cytherea, from thy lamentations for today; no longer beat thy breast: when next year comes, thou wilt have to weep and wail again" (Bion, *Lament for Odonis* pp.97–8).

Historical evidence

This quality of history makes it very unsatisfactory both to the logician and the physical scientist. Heinz Zahrnt begins his book *The Historical Jesus* with an amusing picture of Ernst Troeltsch rising to his feet in a meeting in 1896, and crying aloud, "Gentlemen, everything is tottering", referring of course to the re-emergence of the historical in the field of biblical research. Troeltsch was not a historian but a sociologist. He had been bred in the tradition of the famous remark of Lessing that the contingent verities of history cannot add up to the certainties of the speculative understanding, from which German thinkers have had such difficulty in liberating themselves. No doubt he felt that the more modest claims of history threatened what he had supposed to be certainty. The historian, on the contrary, will throw up his cap to the ceiling with joy at being liberated from the pseudo-certainties of metaphysics and of dogmatic theology into the freedom of his own realm of empiricism and probability. In the field of *annals*, the bare recording of events, it is possible to approach certainty nearly as perfect as that of the scientist. I cannot imagine anyone doubting that King John really did make his mark on Magna Carta on 15th June, 1216. Once we begin to ask why John gave his consent, and what the sixty-one clauses of the charter are supposed to amount to, and what it means that *Ecclesia Anglicana* is to be *libera*, difficulties begin to thicken. Historical evidence is often contradictory. There are immense gaps in it. Moreover, the material is so vast and the questions that can be asked so endless, that some process of selection is inevitable and different pictures of the same events may well emerge. No one can write history today as though Karl Marx had never lived; but Gibbon and Macaulay will never be out of date. This multiplicity is no bad thing. In the very first book that I ever published, I pointed out that anything which exists three-dimensionally cannot be adequately represented unless drawn from at least four angles. Is it purely fortuitous that four Gospels have survived? The historian is content with probability; he refines within the probabilities, but knows that an element of error will always be there, and so the work of the historian can never cease. But Troeltsch was wrong in thinking that all things totter. They do sway a little, but so does the Empire State Building. And no Anglican will be worried by probability, since Bishop Butler has taught us that probability is the law of life.

But there are good historians and bad historians. The great problem in all work in biblical or systematic theology is that the practitioner needs to be expert in three different fields—philology, philosophy and history. These three are very different from one another. I do not think that anyone has ever reached the highest distinction in all three; most of us do not attempt to go beyond two. It is greatly to be regretted that so few of those who write on New Testament subjects have had any training in the art and science of history. The last German well qualified in history, who has written on the New Testament, was Eduard Meyer, the third volume of whose *Ursprung und Anfänge* appeared in 1921. It thus coincided with the beginnings of what came to be known in English as form criticism; in consequence it seems to me that its merits have never been rightly appreciated, and the book was never translated into English. Among English writers in this field, the best historian was probably the admirable Quaker, H. G. Wood, who wrote too little on New Testament subjects, but all of whose work is marked by a refined delicacy of understanding. It was my great good fortune to be trained in the austere atmosphere of the Cambridge school of ancient history, and to have as my special period in Roman history the reigns of Claudius and Nero (A.D. 41–68), just the period of the activity of Saul of Tarsus. When Mr. Robert Graves has done it all in *I Claudius* and *Claudius the God* it all seems so very simple. Perhaps only those who have wrestled with the monk Xiphilinus, who in the ninth century compiled a synopsis of the *History* of the third-century writer Diodorus Siculus, will realise how much more we know about Jesus of Nazareth and Saul of Tarsus than we do about Claudius and Nero.

The historical Jesus

One of the most notable phenomena in critical research today is the re-emergence of the historical Jesus from the mists of critical uncertainty. It is interesting that in many cases the secular historians treat the traditions more kindly than the theologians, and pay attention to material that the theologian might brush on one side. I can record a most impressive example, from my days as professor in Hamburg, of this attitude of the secular historian. We were celebrating the eleventh centenary of the death of our great archbishop Anskar, the patron of all the funeral parlours in Hamburg. One address was given by a theological professor, correct and a little conventional. He was followed by the professor of mediaeval history, who told us that, in studying again the life of Anskar, he had found himself led to pay special attention to the miracles recorded of the saint. Rather to his surprise he found that these were historical materials not to be neglected, and gave him valuable clues to the psychology of the saint and to the way in which people thought in those days, which he might have completely missed, if he had followed the usual rationalistic pattern of considering only what commends itself to the mind of today as historic fact. As we were leaving the hall, one of my colleagues said to me, "The secular historians have emancipated themselves from the Enlightenment more quickly than the theologians." Professor Michael Grant does not know all that can be known about Jesus of Nazareth; but he knows enough to make him feel it is worthwhile to write a book about him, as also about the apostle Paul.

In relation to Jesus, however, the theologians have not been so very far behind. They really are trying today to tell us what history has to say about him. Several references are made in *The Myth of God Incarnate* to the work of Professor Norman Perrin. I once shocked Professor Perrin very much by saying to him that the historico-critical reconstruction of the life of Jesus had not yet begun. This was, of course, intended as an exaggeration, but it was not altogether void of truth. Perrin's method is now well known. We must eliminate everything that could be derived from the Jewish background or from the experience of the early Church, and then we shall have Jesus as he was. The method is defensible as a start, though it might be handled more dexterously than Perrin himself has done. But this is only a beginning. Why should not Jesus have accepted a good deal from the Jewish background? May not some of the experiences of the disciples also have been experiences of Jesus as he really was? The task of history is not merely to present Jesus recognisably as a Jewish rabbi, but also to make him intelligible as the one from whom the Christian movement had its start. Others have seen Perrin's minimum results as the starting point and not as the final term of research. An excellent example of a positive use of critical criteria is Dr. I. H. Marshall's, *I Believe in the Historical Jesus*.

We are certainly not going back to the old method by which everything in the four Gospels was going to be made to coincide with everything else. The clumsily named redaction-criticism is just the recovery of that which had been lost sight of for fifty years, that each of the four evangelists is a great writer and a great theologian in his own right. And the variety of presentation is just what we should expect, if Jesus really was such a super-Napoleonic figure as the founder of Christianity must have been. Variety there is. Vincent Taylor in his book *The Names of Jesus* lists forty-nine names and titles from the New Testament, and points out that all the centuries have added only one more, the Redeemer. But modern study is more and more drawing our attention to a convergence, not only of the Gospels but of the whole of the New Testament evidence, on a figure who is unlike any other who has existed in human history but is recognisable in all the portraits, and in the many terms and phrases in which the Christian believers tried to express their experience of him. There is a great deal that we shall never know; the writers of the New Testament did not write to satisfy our curiosity, but to challenge us to faith. It is important, moreover, to recall that Rudolf Bultmann was quite right when he told us that no amount of historical research can really bring us into touch with Jesus as the Word of God. The accumulation of historical detail might compel intellectual assent; it could never produce the submission of faith. On the other hand, historical research could undermine the faith as it has been known throughout the centuries. If the final result of critical study was to leave us doubtful whether there is any historical basis for the faith, Christianity would be reduced from the level of a religion of history to that of a religion of ideas, and that is something entirely different.

The 'uniqueness' of Jesus

Jesus, then, as a historical figure, is a most remarkable phenomenon. Are we justified in calling him unique? The question is wrongly set. Each one of us is unique. No man can be a substitute for any other man, though this is more evident in those who stand out as individuals than in those who merge too easily with the crowd. We sometimes obscure the difference by the use of general terms. Jesus belongs to the class of religious leaders. How does he relate to other religious leaders? Is there anything in him which is wholly different from others and presents itself as being of unique value? Here judgments will differ. Many arguments could be produced. I will limit myself to one small thing, which seems to me peculiar, and to which I have found no parallel at all in any other faith. The experience of fellowship with Christ is one of continually deepening penitence. The more clearly we see him, the more clearly we see ourselves, and the sight is not pleasant. The saints are always calling themselves the chief of sinners, and this is infuriating to those who see how extremely good they are. But this is not hypocrisy; it is perfectly sincere. And, *pace* Harry Williams, this is not grovelling. It is merely the expression of delighted astonishment that God should still care about creatures like us. And how do we know that he cares? Because Jesus of Nazareth was like that. But how does Jesus convince us that, because he is like that, we can be sure that God is like that? Could it be true that "he that hath seen me hath seen the Father"? And what does that mean? This is the central problem of Christology, perhaps the starting point for Christological consideration.

Jesus Christ was and is different from everyone else. Is he of universal significance? Again our question has to be rather more precisely set. If the human race is one, then everything we do affects the whole human race. If not, not.

Scientists assume that the universe is one. They cannot prove it; but, since without a single self-consistent universe they could not do the work they do, they find this a convenient assumption to make, and empirically it works out rather well. Now, if this is true, there must be somewhere a central point of the universe. No one has any idea where it is; it might be in this room in which I am writing, though I take leave to regard this as rather improbable.

We ask the parallel question. Is the human race one,

and if so is there a single human history? Again, the answer that it is so cannot be demonstrated. But the fact that all human beings, except the mentally deformed, have articulate speech, that there is no language, not even Basque, which cannot be learnt by other humans, and that miscegenation is possible between all human species yet discovered, suggests that it is so. If so, there is no logical argument against the possibility that there could be a central point in human history, on which all the threads converge and from which all the threads diverge.

Towards a theology of history

I do not myself believe that a philosophy of history, derived from the evidence of history itself, is possible. Interesting as some of these philosophies are, they lack that Archimedean point outside history, from which history can be objectively surveyed. I do believe, however, that a theology of history is possible; it is one of the most startling characteristics of the three great monotheistic religions of the Middle East that they all have a theology of history such as is hardly to be attained without a rather clear understanding of a God who is Life, Purpose and Energy. In the Christian theology of history, the death of Christ is the central point of history; here all the roads of the past converge; hence all the roads of the future diverge.

This is not demonstrable. But let us see what sense it makes of history. The Bible picture of history is one of narrowing down to a point. It starts with the first Adam who is the father of us all, and it ends with the last Adam, who in his single individual person wins the victory for us all. The Gospels do very strongly suggest that, as the story unfolds, Jesus increasingly feels himself to be Israel, the one in whom the whole destiny of Israel is to be fulfilled. He is mankind, in that existential moment of confrontation, when obedience is supremely tested and is supremely vindicated. From that moment on, the roads diverge; this gospel is to be preached to the end of the earth. This divergence is hesitant, uneven, perplexing. It leaves many questions unanswered. We in Ireland do not know why we were a century ahead of the Anglo-Saxons in accepting the gospel, why we were privileged, in the worst days of the Church in the West, to develop so remarkable a Christian culture, why we were allowed to become the great missionary people of the West. Why did Germany come so late into the Christian scheme, Scandinavia and Russia even later? Who can answer such questions?

We can only say that this seems to correspond to God's method of working from the small to the great, in the story of life as in the history of the human race. Abraham is called out of Ur of the Chaldees. "How odd of God to choose the Jews" runs the ditty. Very odd indeed. But God was right. The Old Testament is not in the least like any other ancient religious book. Who would have thought that a race so little gifted artistically in those ancient days would produce the books of Job and Second Isaiah and all the rest of it? And from this race came, in due time, Jesus of Nazareth. The Christian Church began with a huddle of frightened men and women, with all the doors shut for fear of the Jews. No one in the Roman world even knew of their existence or of the new faith that had come into being. Yet God gave to this inconspicuous group such expansive vigour that the process of expansion has gone on to the present day and to the bounds of the earth, so that for the first time in history we are presented with the phenomenon of a universal religion, not in the sense that everyone believes in it, but in the sense that the Christian faith has won converts from every branch of the human race, from speakers of every group of languages, from every level of culture and of religious experience from the sophisticated Brahman and the Confucian mandarin to the poverty ridden Eskimo in the farthest north.

The history of religion: divergence and convergence

Professor Hick rightly notes that the history of civilisation is almost the contrary of the history of religion. We are faced with a long story of divergence. For three thousand years, civilisation was the civilisation of the great rivers. All those civilisations have died. But before they died Greece and Rome had taken over and produced that marvellous civilisation of the West, which in time became the quasi-Christian civilisation which is still with us. Almost contemporaneously the Aryans entered India and built up a very different style of culture. A little later the Chinese entered in with their strangely stable system, and extensions in central Asia, Korea, Japan and southeast Asia. Islam has deep roots in both Judaism and Christianity, but has evolved a culture so different from either that it must be classed as the fourth of the great social and religious systems of the world. For many centuries these systems lived in almost total ignorance of one another and of the Christian West, Buddhism alone having an international character.

Now at last divergence is being replaced by convergence. We are being driven into awareness of one another. Juxtaposition does not always lead to tranquillity. Yet the United Nations Organisation, with all its frailty and ineffectiveness, does stand for something. And there is a common language of science which leaps unhindered across all barriers of race, culture and political affiliation. Inevitably the question arises whether there is a common language of religion, whether we should recognise the reality of religious plurality in Britain and elsewhere, and work towards a mutual recognition of religions, as being each in its own sphere a valid and satisfactory way to God, so that religions can co-exist peacefully, as the nations should be able to co-exist politically, without mutual aggression and the attempt to convert believers from one form of religious faith to another.

The idea is attractive. Can it work? We have to be

realistic and recognise that of the great religious or quasi-religious systems, Islam, Buddhism and Marxism claim to have the whole truth and the final word for men. They could not cease from trying to convert others to these faiths without ceasing to be themselves. The adherents of these faiths, when challenged, are quite honest in admitting that this is so. Some Christians hold that some combination of Christianity with Marxism (in praxis, if not in philosophy) or of Christianity with Hinduism is possible. Such a claim is not generally admitted by the convinced adherents of the other faith. Of course there must be profound mutual respect, a desire to learn and to understand, to be enriched by the faith and the experiences of other ages and other climes. Of course there must be co-existence in the sense that frontiers are observed and that no one faith attempts by force or fraud to subvert another. Is it really possible to go further than this?

The propriety of religious conversion

A number of writers at the present time seem completely to overlook the war of the minds. This warfare is less obvious than the war of bodies; but it is more intense, more continuous, more ruthless than the other. In this warfare there is no truce, and we are all engaged in it. A. N. Whitehead sketched out this hidden but ever present reality in his book *Adventures of Ideas*; even he did not perhaps go as far as he might have gone. It is just the fact that religions do die out. Many experience a nostalgia for the past, and sentimentally we can enter into it. But it is simple fact that there are no Gnostics or Manicheans or worshippers of Mithras in the world today, though there are, of course, subterranean survivals from these ancient cults. No one today worships Zeus or Hera or Apollo, for killing truth has glared on them. Jesus Christ was destroyer no less than saviour; at one fell swoop he swept away the whole of the Jewish ritual and ceremonial law; we no longer offer animal sacrifices, and the Epistle to the

Hebrews has plainly told us why we do not. Few people today would be found to defend slavery, though it is still permitted in a number of Muslim states. The British government in India is generally approved for having put down human sacrifice (the Meriah) among the Khonds in south-east India. Not all nations have signed the universal declaration of human rights, since some do not admit that deviationists have any rights, human or divine; but the fact that such a declaration exists must be regarded as registering a measure of convergence in ideas of human dignity. But the warfare of ideas and beliefs is still there.

In all these discussions the voice which is all too rarely heard is that of the convert. Some of our writers seem to feel that the convert is too disreputable a person to have a right to speak. Yet it is the fact that each year a large number of adherents of other faiths do declare themselves to be believers in Jesus and therefore to be no longer adherents of another faith, having discovered that the claims of Jesus are absolute and do not admit of any rival. (There is also the phenomenon of conversion *from* Christian faith to another faith.) Mahatma Gandhi condemned any such conversion, basing his view apparently on the Hindu idea of predestination. If you are a Hindu, that is the will of God for you, and to attempt to become anything else is sheer disobedience to the declared will of God. It is interesting that Gandhi's friend C. F. Andrews, who was by no sense an orthodox Christian and went very far in the direction of peaceful co-existence with Hindus, here directly contradicted his friend, and expressed his judgment that the idea of conversion is necessarily present in any religion which claims to be the truth. But, whether we approve or disapprove, the converts are there. What are we to make of them?

It is not easy to answer the question, since we would like to have a great deal more evidence than we have. Converts are often inarticulate, and have no vocabulary in which to analyse their feelings and their experiences.

Often when they do write they adopt the pious phrases that they have learned from their Christian friends, and this causes their accounts to lose precision. We do have such excellent sources as Dewan Bahadur Appasamy Pillai's *Fifty Years' Pilgrimage of a Convert*, and Bishop Dehqani Tafti's delightful *Design of my World*; also the splendidly naïve biography of Narayan Vaman Tilak by his wife, *I Follow After*. R. Allier's *Psychologie de la Conversion* deals almost exclusively with Africa and is too much schematised in the pattern of the thought of the French psychologist Janet. Fr. Jarrett-Kerr has made a good start with his *Patterns of Christian Acceptance*. But we need a great deal more evidence than we have; and, when the evidence is in, we need a very careful theological analysis of what has been found. If Professor Hick would spend the next ten years working in this much neglected field of theology, and at the end of that time would produce the great book, which he certainly has the capacity to write, he would be rendering a conspicuous service to the cause of inter-faith relations and of Christian clarity.

I wrote 'clarity' and not 'charity'. It seems to me that such confusion has been introduced into the discussion by the use of the word 'salvation', and, especially by the Roman Catholics, of the non-English word 'salvific'. No one today is likely to deny the concern of God for all nations, and the operations of the wisdom of God far beyond the identifiable limits of the Christian fellowship. But in the New Testament the term 'salvation' is used of a particular relationship to God through Jesus Christ which is quite distinct from any other, and clarity would be helped if this usage could be maintained. It is of this Paul writes, when he declares, "I count everything sheer loss, because all is far outweighed by the gain of knowing Christ Jesus my Lord, for whose sake I did in fact lose everything. I count it so much garbage, for the sake of gaining Christ and finding myself incorporate in him" (Phil. 3.8–9, N.E.B.). These words are repeated again and again by converts today. Paul had everything, the very best that Judaism could offer, and yet he counted all that as nothing. What is it that the contemporary convert has found in Jesus Christ that drives him to face exclusion, obloquy, peril, isolation, entrance into an alien world which he often finds sadly cold and unwelcoming? Why is it that he so rarely speaks of his former religion as a preparation for the gospel, and much more often as a hindrance, as a world of darkness, from which he has escaped with great joy? Many would answer precisely that they have found here a *salvation* such as they have not found anywhere else, and that therefore they must run to receive it, whatever may be the cost.

A personal statement

Throughout the book *The Myth of God Incarnate* there runs the repeated suggestion that those who do not follow the writers in their speculations fail to do so because they are too deeply imbedded in ancient traditions to be able to think afresh, or perhaps that they are unwilling to do so. This, I think, is unworthy of the eminent writers. The ideas they put forward have long been before the Churches, though of course their learning offers us some new information, and some new insights into truth from which we are glad to learn. But I am only one of many who have had before them for many years all the problems dealt with in this book, and have reached independently conclusions different from those here set forth. I may perhaps justify this statement by indicating how I have come to be personally involved in all these problems.

In 1922/3 I was studying the New Testament intensively, with special reference to the Hellenistic background. I am rather surprised to recall the books which I read at that time in German—Bousset, Johannes Weiss, Wrede, Eduard Meyer, and of course Reitzenstein, not knowing that I was preparing myself for a future career as a professor in a German University. Then I wrote a fellowship dissertation on the interaction between Neo-platonism and patristic thought in the fourth century. How few helps we had in those days in the study of Plotinus compared with the wealth available today. I wrote then that a number of the fathers were great letter-writers, especially Basil and Augustine (and perhaps I should add that very unpleasant fellow Jerome), and that we cannot know them unless we encounter them not merely as thinkers but also as pastors. If I were writing today, I would add the immense power of the classical liturgies, and the importance of the preachers, especially Augustine and Chrysostom at their best. I have never again in my life worked so hard; but I do not regret the exhausting labour of that expedition into patristic thought.

In 1924 I went to India as a missionary. This involved two further forms of education. First learning to express Christian truth in the simplest possible form for the simple Christians among whom much of my time was spent. Second, immersing myself in Tamil, a most difficult language, and in the whole course of Hindu thought from the Rig Veda to the contemporary Hindu reformers, with special reference to the Saiva Siddhanta, the Tamil form of *bhakti* religion. In later years fate has made me an historian. In writing my *History of Christian Missions* I have had to follow in detail the course of the contacts of Christian faith with other faiths, from Ramon Llull through Robert de Nobili down to J. N. Farquhar and Kraemer, and others whom I do not mention since they are still happily with us. Of course I have learnt many new things and still go on learning. I think that we have only made a beginning in re-thinking all our theology in fully personal terms and that there is still very much to be done. This is the area in which the fathers and the mediaeval scholastics and the reformers were all weak, as I think will be evident to any reader of the Thirty-Nine Articles of the Church of England, to which a great many Anglican ordinands give their general assent every year. But that is a subject for another and longer article.

Being of a radically sceptical temper, I still wake up on about three mornings a week, saying, "Of course it couldn't possibly be true." But then common sense comes to my rescue, saying, "Who are you to decide what is and what is not possible in this wonderful world that God has given us?" So, to my great annoyance, I find myself singing, "Thou only art holy, thou only art the Lord; thou only, O Christ, with the Holy Ghost art most high in the glory of God the Father."

CHAPTER FOUR

Jesus and Later Orthodoxy

CHRISTOPHER BUTLER

CHRISTIANITY TOOK ITS birth from a fact, the fact of the resurrection of Jesus of Nazareth. This fact stands behind every page of the New Testament. Without that fact, there would have been no New Testament, no Christianity. But for that fact, in all probability we should never have heard of the existence of Jesus. It was his resurrection that sparked off a movement and created a new religious grouping, the Church of God, which spread like wildfire across the Mediterranean world and in a few centuries established itself at the centre of the great civilisation that had cradled its birth and then sought to suppress it.

Born of that fact, Christianity had however been conceived with no vocabulary of its own. It had a message to proclaim, but no words of its own with which to express that message. In the New Testament we can see some of the titles, phrases, concepts with which it struggled to express the truth, beyond language, of a new dimension that had come into history, a new order of reality of which the risen Jesus was the centre, the focus, the creative source.

We read the New Testament as if it were a single book. But in reality it is a collection of books, written in different places by a variety of authors, all inspired by the common faith of the first and second generations of Christians. We seek to reach, behind the pages of those books, the earlier (and earliest) attempts to put Christianity and its message into words.

The earliest Christian confessions

It looks as if the first attempt, made in Jerusalem itself soon after the resurrection, picked up and utilised the Jewish religious title, Messiah, Christ, the Anointed of God. But 'Messiah', though a useful and opportune title for the nonce, was at once too vague and too constricting for the message it had to convey. And what could it mean to the non-Jewish converts who shortly began to stream into the Church?

Another title was 'Lord', and this goes back, so far as we can judge, to times not so far removed from those first months in Jerusalem. 'Jesus is Lord' was the profession of faith that entitled one to be baptised. It was a pregnant title and its potentialities were quickly appreciated. Paul's Epistle to the Philippians was written about twenty-five years after the resurrection of Christ. It includes what is thought to be a hymn already in use in the Church when Paul cited it for his own purposes. In this hymn—if such it was—the crucified and now exalted Jesus is assigned the worship of the whole of creation, in terms used in the Book of Isaiah to describe the worship that is reserved to the one and only God of the whole universe:

Philippians 2.9–11	*Isaiah 45.21ff*
Therefore God has highly exalted him and bestowed on him *the name which is above every name*, that at the name of Jesus *every knee should bow*, in heaven and on earth, *and every tongue confess that Jesus is the Lord*, to the glory of God the Father.	Who told this long ago? Who declared it of old? *Was it not I, the Lord? ... I am God, and there is no other.* By myself I have sworn. *To me every knee shall bow, every tongue shall swear.*

There is another title, taking us back probably to the prayer life, and thereby to the self-consciousness of Jesus himself. We read that he addressed his prayers to 'Abba', 'my Father'. It is significant that Jesus is never recorded as having used the term 'our Father' so as to include his followers with himself on equal terms in this relationship. He teaches *them* to pray to 'Our Father in heaven', but he does not include himself with them in this 'Our'. If God was in a unique sense the Father of Jesus, then Jesus was in a unique sense 'the Son of God'. According to Acts, it was this title, Son of God, that Paul used of Jesus from his conversion onwards, to proclaim and recommend his new-found faith. It recurs in the Gospels of Matthew, Mark and Luke and in the Epistle to the Hebrews (whose author was not Paul). Its meaning is central to the argument of the Fourth Gospel.

Jewish message in Greek dress

Though written in Greek, the New Testament books reflect the minds of Jewish Christians. Paul himself, "the apostle of the Gentiles", was a Jew by birth and a Pharisee by education. It has often been argued that the Fourth Gospel is a rendering into Greek concepts of the Christian message—though the case for this can hardly be based on anything more than the opening Prologue of the Gospel. This Prologue uses the concept of the 'Word' of God in order to explain the double relationship of Jesus to God and to man. There was indeed a strong Greek tradition of the 'word' or 'reason' (the Greek word *logos* can mean either) that expresses itself in the whole panorama of existence. But the real roots of the Fourth Gospel's thinking would seem to be the Old Testament teaching of the almighty word of God that created the universe and revealed God's effective will through the prophets.

Thus the new religion that thrust itself out into the non-Jewish world of the Roman Empire took with it a theological background and apparatus which were alien to the thought forms of Graeco-Roman antiquity. We are aware of the problems it had to face, since we in our day have been carrying the Christian faith, long acclimatised to European ways of thinking, to African and Asiatic populations where the tradition of thought is very different. The missionary has to tackle the task of making the old faith indigenous in a new culture. That was the task of the Church in the centuries following the fall of Jerusalem and the death of the last of the apostles.

Greek philosophy had concentrated upon the central issue of 'being', and it had located 'being in itself' at a level above both space and time, and therefore remote from history and 'becoming'. But Jewish thought had been profoundly historical from the start and remained so throughout, at least in its central Palestinian tradition. God, for the Jews, was seen less as the ultimate explanation of everything other than himself than as the One who had manifested his will, his power, his wisdom and mercy, in the great acts of God that marked Israelite history, from the Exodus through the establishment of the Davidic monarchy to the Babylonian captivity and the subsequent restoration of Jewish nationhood and the Temple worship. This great story in which God was the supreme actor and hero was not yet concluded. There was still a Day of the Lord to expect, a re-establishment of the divine authority after the defeat of all the enemies and oppressors of God's people. The Greek philosophers looked *upwards* towards a timeless deity above the cosmic spheres. The Jewish believers looked *forwards* to a God who would ultimately reveal his power in an act that would end all mundane history, the *eschaton* or final divine triumph.

Myth—and truth

How would this Jewish theology look to the eyes of a Greek philosopher? It would seem to be, and indeed it was, a *story*. 'Once upon a time' God had created the visible world and the invisible denizens of heaven. He had also created man, and man had lost his privileges as the 'image and likeness' of God by falling to temptation. But God had not deserted man. Rather, he had chosen a people to be both the recipients of his special favour and his witnesses to an unbelieving world. Into this story the Christians had inserted Jesus, the Messiah, the Lord, the Son of God, the Word of God incarnate, who had mysteriously anticipated and forelived the final *dénouement* of history through his ignominious death and his astounding resurrection.

It was, no doubt, the most beautiful and the most sublime story ever told. But it remained a story—or what the Greeks called a 'myth' (the word has no sinister overtones in Greek. A myth was a story; whether it was a true story or not was not determined by the word used to describe it).

Greek philosophy was expert at dealing with stories. The Greeks were great story-tellers. They had been so since long before Homer and remained so in the age of the great Greek tragedians. But Greek philosophy had been unable to verify the stories—any of them—as they stood. Perhaps the stories incorporated the wisdom of the ages, but they needed criticism; they had to be purified and finally adjusted to the surer teaching of philosophy. In short, the myths had to be demythologised; and the method used was allegorical interpretation. The myths were regarded by the philosophers as being what modern literary critics call *romans à clef*—stories that did not mean what on the surface they said, but something more profound; and philosophy could give you the key to their correct understanding.

If the Church was to convert the Graeco-Roman world, it had, sooner or later, to respond to the challenge of Greek philosophy. For this challenge, though Greek in its provenance, was really the challenge of the human intellect itself, an intellect that is orientated towards the real truth of 'being' as surely as the human heart is orientated towards total bliss. Was the Christianised Jewish story really 'true'? Or was it, at best, a *roman à clef*, a myth in the derogatory sense of the word, a fairy story and a wish-fulfilment dream that must be either rejected *in toto* or at least 'allegorised' to fit the austere requirements of philosophy?

The New Testament writers are quite sure, and the Church herself, before and after the writing of those books, had been and remained quite sure, that the Christian story was true and not just a fairy story. Truth, the very reality of God's abiding trustworthiness and his effective self-revelation, is a dominant theme of the Fourth Gospel. Paul was only stating the general Christian conviction when he affirmed, of the most astounding of all the elements in the story, that "if Christ be not risen, then we are false witnesses of God; then you remain unforgiven, unredeemed; we Christians are of all men the most wretched"—because we have put our final faith in a lie.

Arius and Nicaea

What the New Testament books themselves did not do, what remained to be done in the centuries from A.D. 100 to A.D. 451 (the date of the Council and Formula of Chalcedon) was to meet philosophy head on and respond to its legitimate requirements, while steadfastly refusing to accept (along with ancient Greek religion and the mystery religions of early Christian times) the offer of an allegorical explanation of Christianity and its eventual assimilation to 'comparative religion'.

The issues were first brought to a head, and to official cognisance at the highest level, by the theological speculations of a Christian priest of Alexandria, Arius by name. For philosophy, the 'scandal' of Christianity was the Church's worship—in the full sense of that term—of the man Jesus. Arius suggested that Jesus, while no doubt the highest being *under* God, was not actually himself divine; he was indeed the Word of God, but that Word was itself a creature—the creature above all other creatures—to be sure, but still not prior to all creation. He was indeed the "wisdom" of God, but an Old Testament text—as translated into Greek—affirmed that God "created" wisdom "in the beginning of his ways" (Prov. 8.22).

This theology the Council of Nicaea (A.D. 325) firmly rejected. In order to exclude it, they affirmed that Jesus, the Son of God, is 'consubstantial' with his divine Father. The word was unscriptural, but the Council accepted it as a correct interpretation of the meaning of the New Testament. Not only was the word unscriptural; it was philosophic. The official Church thus took the first step towards genuine dialogue with philosophy. Unfortunately the word, while adequate for the intended purpose of excluding Arianism, had an undefended flank: it could be exploited in favour of a quite different heresy: the heresy that the Word of God is not really distinguishable from the One whom Jesus prayed to as his Father.

There ensued a century and a quarter of acute and often bitter theological controversy and, incidentally, theological development. One group of Arians (for the heresy did not die immediately) pressed the claims of Greek philosophical logic with such rationalistic fervour that, had they won the day, Christianity would have lost all contact with the ultimate mystery that shrouds God from our earth-bound vision. The orthodox theologians could not accept this; but neither could they refuse to face the issues raised by philosophy. What they did was not to surrender to rationalism but to reshape the vocabulary proffered by the philosophic tradition, and the concepts which that vocabulary expressed, so as both to respect the demands of the human intellect and to preserve the truth as it had been enshrined in the Bible and expounded in the Church's tradition. In particular, the words *ousia* (being or essence), *hypostasis* (substance or subsistence), *physis* (nature) and *prosopon* (person, or self-presentation of a person) were re-examined, refined, distinguished and accommodated to the requirements of the Christian gospel.

Of this whole, lengthy and sometimes tortuous process the outcome was the Formula of Chalcedon.

The Formula of Chalcedon

The Council of Chalcedon was summoned, rather against the wishes of Pope Leo of Rome, by the Roman Emperor (for the 'Great Church' was by now the established religion of the Empire), to settle a dispute engendered by the theology of a certain Eutyches, a not very intelligent theologian of Constantinople who thought that he was a faithful disciple of the late Cyril of Alexandria. Eutyches had no difficulties about the Godhead of Jesus; but he held that, in the incarnation, the 'humanness' of Jesus was completely *absorbed* into his divinity—you could say that this was the opposite extreme from Arius's position, which had been that Jesus, though in a sense human, was not in any real sense divine. Eutyches thought that Jesus was divine, but his explanations seemed to diminish, ultimately exclude, the reality of his humanity.

The Church has lived with the Formula of Chalcedon for over a millennium and a half. It has seen in it a faithful restatement of its own immemorial faith, the faith already articulated in the Prologue of the Fourth Gospel in the doctrine that the Word of God who was himself divine 'became flesh' (i.e. became a real human being) in and as Jesus of Nazareth. The Formula was rejected by one group of near-Eastern churches, including that of Egypt; and these churches have their modern successors in the Coptic and Armenian Orthodox churches of the East. It is a cause for deep thankfulness that today there is virtually complete accord between their theologians and those of the Roman Catholic and Orthodox Communions that the Formula of Chalcedon does in fact express the faith that is common to us all.

This Formula has caused a certain amount of uneasiness among some modern scholars and theologians—curiously enough among men whose professed aim would be to 'demythologise' Christianity. The one thing that the Formula of Chalcedon certainly does *not* do is to indulge in 'myth' in the derogatory sense of that word. It does what is almost precisely the opposite: it makes a decisive—and in my view successful—effort to preserve the intellectual respectability of Christianity against the tendency to treat our fundamental convictions as elements in a fairy story. It would be much more sensible to criticise the Formula as too intellectualist, too academic, too subtle for the common man.

What does the Formula affirm?

Following therefore the holy Fathers, we confess one and the same our Lord Jesus Christ, and we all teach harmoniously [that he is] the same perfect in Godhead, the same perfect in manhood, truly God and truly man, the same of a reasonable soul and body; consubstantial with the Father in Godhead, and the same consubstantial with us in manhood, like us in all things except sin; begotten before the ages of the Father in Godhead, the same in the last days for us and for our salvation [born] of Mary the virgin *theotokos* in manhood, one and the same Christ, Son, Lord, unique; acknowledged in two natures without confusion, without change, without division, without separation—the difference of the two natures being by no means taken away because of the union, but rather the distinctive character of each nature being preserved, and [each] combining in one Person and *hypostasis*—not divided or separated into two Persons, but one and the same Son and only-begotten God, Word, Lord Jesus Christ . . .*

* Translation according to E.R. Hardy, ed., *Christology of the later Fathers*, p. 373; as quoted in Alan Richardson, ed., *A Dictionary of Christian Theology.*

The Formula's meaning and importance

There is a story of a parish priest who, having duly read out to his congregation a pastoral letter from the bishop of the diocese, went on: "And now I will tell you what his lordship was really trying to say." At the risk of being accused of doing likewise, I venture to suggest that this long and complicated formula is affirming above all two things. First, that Christianity has its source and centre in a historical figure, Jesus of Nazareth, and Jesus is as uniquely himself, single in his reality, as any other historical figure. But second, that we can affirm about this single historical figure a double series of predicates. One series is such as we could predicate of anyone else: that he was fully human, a body-and-soul human being, with a human mother, "like us in all things"—though the Council adds concerning the human Jesus that, while fully human, he was not—like the rest of us—a sinner. The other series of predicates are such as we can only attribute to God—the Council does not specify these predicates, but they were familiar to the Christianised philosophy of the time. They are predicates that attach not only to Jesus but also to his Father and to the Holy Spirit; yet Jesus is not the Father (nor, of course, is he the Holy Spirit)—and the distinction is implied in the affirmation that, precisely in his Godhead, Jesus is "begotten before the ages of the Father".

There can, in my view, be no doubt that this Formula expresses the authentic Christian faith. Jesus is himself and is not schizophrenic or a 'dual personality'. Jesus is the human son of Mary of Nazareth and was crucified under Pontius Pilate. Jesus, nevertheless, is in the strict sense of the term adorable—to be worshipped with a worship that, offered to any save God would be idolatry; in the words that embody the climax of the Fourth Gospel, he is "my Lord and my God".

Then why all the complicated language of the Formula? To answer this question fully we should have to review in detail the intricate theological disputes and debates preceding the Council of Chalcedon. I can understand that this complication and the consequent prolixity are displeasing to some. But when a series of questions have been raised about a highly mysterious reality, it is not always easy to answer them all in a single brief and simple statement—is it possible to be brief and simple about the electron? In short, as regards what the Chalcedonian Fathers meant to affirm, it is clear that this was precisely the traditional faith, and that they succeeded in doing this in terms of their own age. As for today, and in reply to orthodox theologians who dislike the Formula, I feel inclined to say (echoing Bruce Bairnsfather's immortal soldier in his shell-hole on the Western front): "If you know of a better Formula, go to it."

The Formula has been criticised also because it leaves out so much of the ethical and spiritually elevating content of the gospel. In other words, it is not too long, but too short. The simple answer to this objection is that the Council of Chalcedon was concerned to protect the gospel faith against certain particular attacks; it was not concerned to rewrite, or to expound, the whole gospel. Our faith is in a Person with a history that is uniquely his; we assent to the Formula of Chalcedon because, if we deny its truth, we deny the very reasons why this Person is indeed our Saviour, our Brother, and our Lord.

The real issue today is whether or not we *can* believe in Christianity. Those who reject the Formula of Chalcedon are, almost without exception, men who have in fact answered that question for themselves in the negative. Christian faith has, in a sense, never been easy. Paul says that its centre-piece, the crucifixion of the Anointed of God, is a scandal to the Jews and a matter for derision to the Gentiles. Why is this faith, for us who believe, the very 'power of God'? To answer this would require not the closing paragraph of a short essay, but a book. Let me say one thing.

The reasons of the intellect deserve respect; but so also do 'the reasons of the heart'. Greek philosophy has shown us the way to the notion of God as the answer to the ultimate questionings of our intellect. Christianity has accepted that way and the compelling nature of its goal. But man is more than a computer. He has a heart. He has a fundamental hunger for what is good and holy. The Christian gospel adds to what philosophy has told us. Briefly, it has revealed to us that God is love, and that God, being love, loves us tiny and imperfect creatures; loves us in our individuality and loves us collectively, loves man the person and man the collective on pilgrimage through the epochs of temporal history. Love's impulse is to help the beloved by identification with his concerns, and with himself. Christianity teaches us that God so loves us that not only *would* he, if necessary, identify himself with our destiny and our fate in order to lead us to a triumph beyond that fate, but that he *has actually* done so. This is the meaning of the 'incarnation'. This is what makes the orthodox Christian creed not only a sublime monument of human thought but the key to human hope and the challenge to us to respond, by the grace of God the Holy Spirit, to the appeal of divine love. As Augustine tells us, we were made for God and our heart is restless till it comes to repose in him. We cannot by our own unaided powers bridge the gulf between divine love and our human limitations. Jesus of Nazareth, the incarnate Word of God, has bridged the gulf; and that Word is a word of divine wooing of us in our human weakness and our need.

CHAPTER FIVE

Jesus, God Incarnate

Brian Hebblethwaite

The importance of the incarnation

The Christian doctrine of the incarnation is one of the two central doctrines which set out the *unique* features of Christian faith in God. Christianity shares with some other religions belief in an infinite and transcendent God, the source of the world's being and of all its values. It recognises that in every part of the world, traditions of religious belief and religious experience have made it possible for men and women to enjoy the blessedness of spiritual life and of the knowledge and love of God. But the Christian doctrine of the incarnation expresses the conviction of Christians that this God has made himself known fully, specifically and personally, by taking our human nature into himself, by coming amongst us as a particular man, without in any way ceasing to be the eternal and infinite God.

The other central doctrine is that of the Trinity. The reason why the doctrines of the incarnation and Trinity go together is partly a matter of history and partly a matter of rational reflection. It was because the early Christians, in the light of the resurrection of Jesus from the dead, came to recognise his divinity and to experience him as the self-revelation of God, that they perceived the necessity of believing that God himself, in his own being, exists in an internal relationship of love given and love received. That love, they saw, was mirrored in the relationship of Jesus to the Father. That same love they experienced in their own lives: not only was it poured out upon them but it was a relationship in which they too were caught up and came to share. But they also came to realise that the very notion of a God who is Love requires us to think in terms of an internally differentiated and relational deity.

This may sound complicated, but the essence of the matter is quite simple. On the one hand we admit the greatness and transcendence of God. No religious mind can deny the ultimate mystery of God. The richness of his inner being far surpasses our powers of comprehension. On the other hand we believe that this mysterious and ineffable God, out of pure love for mankind, has made himself known to us, in the most direct and comprehensible way possible, by coming amongst us as one of us, and sharing our life, its heights and depths, its joys and sorrows.

To believe in God incarnate, then, is to believe that God has chosen *this* way of making himself known and drawing us to himself. The doctrine involves taking very seriously both the divinity and the humanity of Jesus Christ. While it is primarily a doctrine about God, so that God himself, in one of the modes of his eternal being, is to be thought of as the subject of all the predicates we use in speaking of Jesus Christ, nevertheless the doctrine also asserts the real humanity of Jesus. In no way do we follow the 'docetic' tendencies of early Christianity, which found it hard to believe, for example, that Jesus shared the limitations of human psychology and knowledge. In other words, the incarnation involved God's subjecting himself to the limitations of real humanity in order to achieve his purposes of revelation and reconciliation.

According to this doctrine of the incarnation, the man Jesus cannot be thought of apart from his being God incarnate. Or rather, so to think of him is to abstract from the full reality of what was taking place at that time in history. Jesus was not just a particularly good man whom God decided to adopt. The whole story of God's relation to the world pivots around his personal presence and action here in our midst in Jesus Christ.

The implications of the incarnation

The moral and spiritual force of this doctrine is very great. In the first place we can see that God in Christ takes upon *himself* responsibility for all the world's ills. God bears the brunt of suffering and evil by subjecting *himself* to their cruelty and horror. By so doing, he reveals, as he could in no other way, the reality and depth and costly nature of his forgiving love. And by this identification of himself with us and our predicament he draws us to himself in an utterly moral and personal way.

In the second place it is the personal presence of God this side of the divide between infinite and finite that shows us who he is and what he is like. By this act, God overcomes the vagueness and the dread that limit the experience of God which elsewhere and otherwise men can and do enjoy. If Jesus is God *in person*, then our knowledge of God has an intelligible personal human focus. In Jesus' character and acts we see the character and acts of God himself in terms we can readily understand. At the same time God does not overwhelm us by his self-revelation. Instead he invites and wins our personal response.

This presence and action of God, here in our midst in person, cannot be thought of as a repeatable affair. If God is one, only one man can *be* God incarnate. Several people can manifest similar general characteristics and thus, perhaps, illustrate certain general truths about God's nature. But Jesus is *the* human face of God. The doctrine of the incarnation is emptied of its point and value in referring to a real person-to-person encounter if we suppose that a series of human beings from different times, places and cultures were all God incarnate. On such a view, God at once resumes the characteristics of vagueness and dread that the Christian doctrine of the incarnation teaches us to overcome.

The particularity of the incarnation—the fact that if God was to come to us in person it would have to be at a particular time and place in history—certainly involves seeing the whole creation and the whole of human history pivoting upon a brief slice of space-time in the history of the ancient Middle East. It also means that we in the twentieth century and all other human beings at other times and places, however long human history lasts, cannot enjoy precisely the same face-to-face human encounter with God incarnate that the disciples and other contemporaries of Jesus in Palestine enjoyed. Our personal dealings with God are through the spiritual and sacramental presence of the risen and ascended Christ. But the point remains that this is the spiritual and sacramental presence of the one who did tread the hills of Palestine, whose character and acts we read about in the Gospels. Again it needs to be stressed that the spiritual sense of the presence of God here and now requires this human focusing in the Jesus of Nazareth of nearly two thousand years ago, if we are to enjoy the precision and clarity of God's self-disclosure through incarnation. Not that the humanity of God is a thing of the past only. The risen Christ's glorified humanity is, we believe, permanently taken into God, though it is not manifested to us at present—that is part of our future expectation. But for the present it is by his spiritual and sacramental presence that Jesus becomes *our* contemporary and reveals God to us here and now.

The possibility of the incarnation

To suppose that God can and does relate himself to us and make himself known to us in this particular way, over and above the intimations of his reality and nature which religion in general provides, does, of course, imply that it is *possible* for him to do so. But who are we to say that the nature of God Almighty, the infinite and eternal ground of our being, is such as to render this impossible? On the contrary, Christianity has taught us to see God's power specifically made known in the weak human life of Jesus, his eternity in the temporal span of Jesus' life, his inner trinitarian relations in the prayers of Jesus to the Father and the gift of the Spirit to the Church. We have no basis at all for saying that God *cannot*, without ceasing to be God, unite his creation to himself primarily in an incarnate life, and then derivatively in and through our response to the risen and ascended one.

When we reflect on the historical evidence for these remarkable but central doctrines of Christianity, we need to beware of thinking that historical evidence alone must be seen to *necessitate* such an interpretation before we can allow ourselves to accept it. Of course the historical facts must be seen to *allow* or even to *suggest* this interpretation, if it is to be at all credible. We have to do justice to the impression made by Jesus, to the belief in his resurrection, and to the rapid growth of 'high' Christologies. But historical evidence alone cannot compel assent. We have also to reckon with Christian experience of the risen Christ down the ages, including that of our friends and of ourselves. And particularly, I think, we need to rediscover what I have called the moral and spiritual force of the doctrine of the incarnation, the sense it makes of the relation between God and his creation, and the anticipations it yields, together with the doctrines of the resurrection and ascension, of the ultimate destiny of God's creation.

Current theological scepticism on these matters results from a narrowness of vision, an attempt to see the world as it is now construed in the natural and human sciences as being related tangentially to a mysterious, hidden and extremely vague, divine ground or spirit. But the theologian must stick to his last. A theist is one who sees all

CHAPTER SIX

Jesus and Historical Scepticism

MICHAEL GREEN

IN THESE DAYS, when every article of the creed is challenged by some who profess to believe it, and when the scepticism of professors of theology is sometimes tantamount to atheism, it is not surprising that many people are deeply puzzled. What is left of the Christian faith? What are we expected to believe?

It seemed worth while therefore in this chapter to attempt to clarify the situation. I shall not attempt to 'prove' any article of the Christian faith. What I shall try to do is to expose some of the underlying presuppositions behind much of the current scepticism in theological circles; then to ask whether there is compelling reason to suppose that excessive scepticism about Jesus of Nazareth is warranted; and finally to examine some of the consequences that follow from adopting sceptical presuppositions.

I. THE ASSUMPTIONS BEHIND HISTORICAL SCEPTICISM ABOUT JESUS

There is no divine element in the Bible

One of the analogies frequently used by writers in *The Myth of God Incarnate* runs something like this. In the last century adventurous theologians rescued the Church from biblical fundamentalism. What we are doing is to rescue the Church from credal fundamentalism. We no longer believe that everything recorded in the Bible is literally true—so runs the argument: why should we believe that fourth-century credal formulations about Jesus being of the same nature as the Father are literally true? Both Professor Wiles and Professor Hick use this analogy. It is worth asking ourselves whether it holds water.

The doctrine of Scripture taught from the earliest days in the Church was that Scripture had a dual authorship; men spoke, but God spoke through them (2 Pet. 1.21). Their writings embodied all the accidental qualities imposed by the historical situation of the authors, their cultural background and literary skills. But their writings also embodied the Word of God speaking in and through the human authors (complete with their historical, cultural and linguistic limitations). It has always been recognised that there is in Scripture a wide variety of literary genres: poetry, prose, history, wisdom literature, parable and allegory, apocalypse and epistle. To give every part the monochrome, equal evaluation of literalness is nowhere demanded by the Bible itself and is plainly unimaginative and foolish. But to reject literalism is one thing: quite another is to throw out the divine overruling of the biblical writers, and assume that the Bible is just like any other book. Now that is precisely what has happened in many scholarly quarters. It is assumed that "both in form and content the Bible entirely shares the laws which govern secular literature" (James Barr in *S.J.T.*, May 1958). Whatever those iron laws may be we are entitled to wonder. But Professor Barr makes himself very explicit in the following quotation from *The Bible in the Modern World* (p.120):

My account of the formation of the biblical tradition is an account of a *human* work. It is *man's* statement of his beliefs, the events he has experienced, the stories he has been told, and so on. It has long been customary to align the Bible with concepts like Word of God, or revelation, and one effect has been to align the Bible with a movement *from God to man*.

It is man who developed the biblical tradition and man who decided when it might be suitably fixed and made canonical. If one wants to use the Word of God type of language, the proper term for the Bible would be Word of Israel, Word of some leading Christians.

What has happened is this. Whilst setting out to correct literalism, liberal scholars have driven out the divine element altogether from the Bible. It is no longer Word of God, but word of men, and singularly unreliable word at that.

Something analogous is happening with the doctrine of the incarnation in the hands of reductionist theologians. What they profess to be doing is the very proper task of questioning the literalness of the Chalcedonian definition of our Lord's two natures, and seeking to reinterpret Christology in a philosophical framework that rings true in the modern world, as talk of 'substance' and 'hypostasis' does not. All very right and proper. But what in fact they seem to be doing, at least in the recent symposium, is to evacuate the divine element from Jesus just as surely as they have done it with Scripture. They are denying not merely Nicene and Chalcedonian definitions of Christ but the basic truth which these definitions sought, in the cultural heritage of their own day to express, that Jesus shared the nature of God as well as our nature. They are not reinterpreting traditional Christology but abandoning it.

The whole of our book is concerned with the Christological question. But let me pause for a moment on the biblical question. When Professor Barr opts to take the view he does of Scripture he is, of course, perfectly entitled to do so, but he is not entitled to claim that his view is necessarily involved in the historical-critical method. The scientific and historical study of Scripture does not make a man conservative or liberal any more than the scientific and historical study of economics makes a man a Marxist or a Tory.

Nor, I think, can he claim that his view can properly be called a Christian one, for three reasons. In the first place, the Bible does not give this account of itself. On almost every page we find the claim that God is active in revealing himself to his people. "Thus says the Lord", "the Lord spoke to Moses, saying . . ." and the like are claims that are everywhere apparent. The apostles in the New Testament days seem as clear as the prophets of old that they were speaking under the direct inspiration of the Holy Spirit (e.g. Gal. 1.6–12, 1 Thess. 2.13, 1 Pet. 1.11f, 1 Cor. 2.16, 14.37, 1 John 1.1–5, 2 John 10, 2 Tim. 3.16, Rev. 22.18f). Very properly, Professor Barr acknowledges that the account he gives of the Bible is not the account the Bible gives of itself.

Secondly, Jesus does not give this account of the Bible. He certainly does not regard it as merely the word of man. It is the word of man, but through it breathes the Word of God. "David himself said by the Holy Spirit," he said, quoting Psalm 110 and maintaining the dual authorship (Mark 12.36), and again, "the Scripture cannot be broken" (John 10.34). Jesus framed his teaching by it; he based his life and calling upon it. It was the Word of the Lord. This attitude to Scripture remained constant throughout his life from the first sermon at Nazareth until after the resurrection; it is also attested in all four Gospels and the strata like M and Q which underlie them. So Professor Barr is taking issue with Jesus on this matter.

He is also going against the teaching of the Church. The earliest Church engrossed itself in the Scriptures of the Old Testament and saw in them the Christian revelation in prediction, allegory and typology. They soon accorded to the New Testament writings an equal authority, and regarded them as decisive for the Church's belief and practice. Thus Origen can write in the third century, "The sacred books were not the work of men; they were written by the inspiration of the Holy Spirit, at the will of the Father of all, through Jesus Christ" (*de Principiis* 4.9). This view was common coin in the Church, and is reflected in official formularies. The Church of Rome, for instance, follows her own Council of Trent: "The Synod, following the example of the orthodox fathers, receives and venerates all the books of the Old and New Testament, seeing the one God is the author of both" (*Session 4 of the Council of Trent*). The Westminster Confession, the official statement of Dr. Barr's own Presbyterian Church, states: "All the books of the Old and New Testament are given by inspiration of God to be the rule of faith and life."

There it is, then. The Bible writers themselves believed they were inspired by God: Jesus believed they were: the Church believed they were. Some modern scholars do not believe this. The issue is plain. The choice is ours.

There is no possibility of miracle

The second widespread assumption among theological writers is that we live in a closed scientific universe where there is no possibility of miracle. God simply does not act that way. He expresses himself in the regularities of the natural world and any disruption of that ordered pattern of regularity is to be discounted. "Christianity is always adapting into something which can be believed" is a presupposition of the essayists in this symposium; so much so that it is quoted in the first paragraph of the book. And miracles cannot be believed. The miracles of Jesus must be repudiated, because miracles do not happen: so ran the message of the film *Who was Jesus?*, directed by one of the contributors to *The Myth of God Incarnate*.

It is this assumption that makes the contributors uneasy with the idea of incarnation. It would run counter to the natural course of things. It would be an intrusion.

It is this assumption that makes them anxious to dispense with the literal resurrection of Jesus. I mentioned earlier that this is a very modern view. It has not arisen from any fresh study of the New Testament material, but from the presupposition that the miraculous cannot be believed. As Michael Ramsey wrote, "The criticism which rejects the empty tomb as *a priori* incredible or inconsequent or crude has its roots in a philosophy which is far removed from the New Testament. For the gospel in the New Testament involves the freedom of the living God and an act of new creation which includes the bodily no less than the spiritual life of man" (*The Resurrection of Christ*, p.55).

Alan Richardson puts the heart of the matter with great incisiveness: "The notion that the resurrection of Christ was a purely 'spiritual' affair, while his corpse remained in the tomb, is a very modern one, which rests upon theories of the impossibility of miracles drawn from nineteenth century physics" (*An Introduction to the Theology of the New Testament*, p.196).

Several weaknesses in this assumption, which underlies a great deal of the negative reasoning among theologians of the Bultmann school, need to be explored. In the first place, modern science no longer thinks in terms of a closed cause-and-effect universe. Quantum mechanics and the principle of indeterminacy have made it very precarious to argue what may or may not be possible. A great many things that we take for granted today, such as space travel and television, would have been deemed impossible on the presuppositions of nineteenth-century science.

Moreover, the type of argument used by the authors of the symposium professing to believe in a transcendent God but unwilling to believe that he could interfere with the ordering of the world, has about it that air of the 'God of the gaps' that they would be the first to repudiate. For if the world is a closed system, why should we invoke God to account for it? Have we any need of that hypothesis? If we are reduced to a God who is supposed to be the source of our world but is too effete to become involved in it personally, we hang uncertainly between the theists and the atheists, and are of all men the most to be pitied: believers in God, but a God who cannot or will not get involved.

After all, what does the scientific method involve? Top rank scientists do not exclude possibilities *a priori*. They look at the evidence. Our understanding of the universe was not built up by dogmatic assertions of what is and what is not possible, but by patient exploration of what has actually happened in the world. The methodology is empirical. The laws of nature are nothing but a series of observed uniformities. It goes without saying that if a well attested exception to the series of uniformities occurs, the scientist will seek a more all-embracing 'law' to cover both the uniformities and the exception. It was in this way, if I understand it aright, that Einstein's physics proved an improvement on the models used by Newton. Einstein did not simply replace Newton: but his explanations of phenomena accounted both for the material Newton had organised under 'laws' and for the exceptions to those laws which had remained untidy surds on the Newtonian pattern. Similarly, it is perfectly evident to all and sundry that dead men do not rise. Christians were never so naïve as to suppose they did. But that does not mean to say that if we had one example of a perfect, sinless being, he would inevitably be held in thraldom by death. There are no other examples of this species to compare him with. Therefore the scientist will be open to the possibility that Jesus might possibly have risen from the dead, provided only that the evidence is strong enough to warrant it. He will not exclude it without examination. Such a procedure would be quite unscientific. Yet it is the procedure adopted by some modern theologians in the name of science!

In any case, who are we to determine the impossibility

T—E

of God becoming one of us, or of rising from the dead? We shall not be easily convinced that he has done so. We shall scrutinise the evidence with care. No man ought to accept the doctrines of the incarnation and resurrection without having agonised over them, without having started by believing them incredible. But if, after wrestling with the evidence he is persuaded that it is compelling, then there is no *a priori* reason why he should conclude that it is impossible and therefore did not happen! If we believe in a God who is the source of both the physical world and man with all his qualities and values, there is no way in which we can exclude the possibility of his loving us enough to come to us and live among us and die for us and rise for us. It is eminently wonderful, but not quite incredible. And the scientific method has nothing to say against it.

There is no finality about Jesus

The third assumption that lies underneath a good deal of modern reductionism about Jesus is that there are many ways to God, and we must not offend against propriety, let alone against reason, by supposing that Jesus has any finality, or that he represents the only way to God. Is the world not now a cosmic village? Are there not many roads up the mountain to God? Therefore the more we can show that Jesus is just like other religious figures, the better.

There are three factors in particular which have lent support to this very widely held view. The first is the increasing intercourse there is between men of different nationalities and faiths in our shrinking world. The second is an increasing relativism in thought: truth is at a discount, tolerance is the greatest virtue. The third is the failure of Christianity to make much headway among the adherents of the four great faiths of the world, Buddhism, Hinduism, Islam, Judaism and perhaps we should add, Communism. Behind these three reasons there lies a deeper despair, which is profoundly connected with the matter in hand: two world wars and the present world situation give little support to the traditional Christian belief that history is linear, with a beginning and a mid point and a goal. If history is merely "the tale told by an idiot, full of sound and fury, signifying nothing", let us abandon our insistence on its importance, and surrender to mythology and poetic romance.

Despite these blandishments, the way of syncretism is not a viable option for Christians. The scandal of particularity lies at the heart of the religion of Jesus. It was so from the start. "The Jews demand signs and the Greeks seek wisdom, but we preach Christ crucified, a stumbling block to Jews and folly to Gentiles, but to those who are called, both Jews and Greeks, Christ the power of God and the wisdom of God" (1 Cor. 1.22f). The particularity of Christ, the absolute claims made for him, have always constituted a major stumbling block to those who seek salvation through ideas. There is a sense in which much that passes for Christianity today is not Christianity at all but a form of Hinduism. For the Hindu, history is unimportant: the idea is everything. Christianity, I once heard Bishop John Taylor say, is a story religion with theories: Hinduism is a theory religion with stories. And once we lose sight of the particularity of Jesus and salvation through God become man in him, then our faith becomes just one more stream emptying itself in the sea of Hinduism. What survives may make Christian sounding noises, but it will no longer be Christianity. The nerve of the faith, God made manifest in the flesh, will have been cut.

It is salutary to remember that Christianity was born in a world every bit as unified and every bit as pluralistic in matters of faith as our own. The Roman pantheon was most hospitable: additional deities were accorded a ready welcome, so long as you didn't try to be exclusive, or to unseat the favourite gods of others. The early Christians declined the offer. For them Jesus was not one among many but the embodiment of the Only. He was not a divine sort of man but God become man. He endured no mythical labours of Hercules but a literal and agonising cross. He was not deified by decree of the senate but raised by God to the place of power in the universe. Syncretism was out. It was not a Christian option, for if you believed that the Absolute had come into our world, how could you rank him with the relative? The same holds good in the religious pluralism of today.

It is also worth bearing in mind that Christianity was born into a world where much that was true and good was taught by the various philosophical schools such as Neoplatonism, Stoicism, Epicureanism and the like. How were the excellent precepts taught by these good men to be squared with the particular claims made for Jesus? Should Christianity give up its claim to absolute truth? They did not take this option. Instead, so sure were they of the final truth brought them in Christ that the early Christians were very ready to recognise truth and goodness wherever it was to be found. It was all a reflection of that universal *logos* or reason that had taken personal and final form in Jesus of Nazareth. There was nothing narrow about their particularist incarnational faith, nor need there be about ours. It certainly does not lead to the strange conclusion postulated by Dr. Hick:

The problem which has come to the surface in the encounter of Christianity with the other world religions is this: If Jesus was literally God incarnate, and if it is by his death alone that men can be saved, and by their response to him alone that they can appropriate that salvation, then the only doorway to eternal life is the Christian faith. It would follow from this that the large majority of the human race so far have not been saved. But is it credible that the loving God and Father of all men has decreed that only those born within one particular thread of human history shall be saved? (*op. cit.* p.180.)

Professor Hick would have done well to have studied with care Bishop Lesslie Newbigin's book, *The Finality of Christ*. As Bishop in Madras he has long had to wrestle with the problem before us, and his book is one of the most sensitive and profound interpretations of historic Christianity facing a Hindu situation. Newbigin would want to say three things to that quotation from Hick. First, how do you know that God is the "loving God and Father of all men" if he has not disclosed himself as such in Jesus Christ? If there is no *event*, from what do we derive the *idea* of God's loving Fatherhood? Once severed from the event of the incarnation we are at large in the sea of ideas about the divine. Why should we suppose that he is personal, and loving, and the Father of all men?

Second, why should Hick be distressed about the fate of "the large majority of the human race" whilst maintaining that the traditional Christian view of heaven and hell, salvation and loss did not do much harm for a thousand years and more in pre-critical days? In other words, why should the doctrine be more distasteful now than it was then? The answer lies in the numbers involved. And Newbigin will have none of it:

I cannot find anything in the New Testament to support what seems to be a widespread view today, namely that whereas it is tolerable to think of a few people being lost, it is intolerable to think of the majority of mankind being lost. Certainly this is not God's arithmetic according to the parables of Jesus. He is the one who cares for the unique individual, the last and least. I do not find in the New Testament a God who is impressed by majorities, or daunted by monster deputations. I do not find the New Testament grounds for the view that because few Hindus or Muslims are converted to Christianity, therefore the idea of conversion must be abandoned. (*op. cit.* p.114.)

And thirdly, Bishop Newbigin would want to take issue with the notion that to insist on the finality of Jesus Christ for man's salvation means that "the only doorway to eternal life is the Christian faith". It is one thing to claim that all salvation is through Christ, and Christians do say this, even if Professor Hick denies it (p.181). It is quite another to claim that nobody finds life with God unless they pass through the doorway of explicit Christian faith. This is yet another of those inexplicable blunders which spoil Dr. Hick's essay. The Christian Church has never maintained that overt knowledge of the person and work of Jesus was essential for salvation. How could Abraham and the Old Testament saints have been reconciled with God? The Old Testament does not, as is commonly supposed, teach salvation by good works, while the New Testament teaches salvation by faith. Both Testaments maintain the same truth: that God is the only Saviour, and that he approaches men in sheer grace to which the only proper response is adoring faith. Abraham is a good example. He knew nothing of the incarnation or the cross. But he knew that God had set his love upon him and called him: he responded in obedient faith, and stepped out into the desert with no security but El-Shaddai, the God who is enough. But Abraham was not accepted by God because he was a good man, or made sacrifices, or believed. He was accepted because of what God in Christ was going to do for him on Calvary. We are accepted because of what God in Christ has done for us on Calvary. The only difference is that we understand a little more about it. And the Bible leads us to suppose that wherever men rely on the great God to accept them irrespective of their merits they can be accepted by him: not because Hinduism is a pleasing alternative to Christianity but because no man-made religious system, Hindu, Christian, Communist or whatever can bring a finite sinful man into lasting relation with an infinite personal God. The movement both of disclosure and of rescue must be from God to man, not vice versa. And wherever a man relies on God to accept him, he shows himself to be a child of Abraham the archetypal believer. So to maintain with the writer of Acts (whose 'primitive' Christology so appeals to Dr. Hick) that "there is salvation in no one else, for there is no other name under heaven given among men by which we must be saved" (4.12) does not mean that no man can be saved unless he has heard of Jesus: it does mean that Jesus is the only saviour of men. But for a further unpacking of what is meant by salvation in this context, and the difference between becoming an adherent of the Christian religion and believing in Jesus, it would be well to turn to Lesslie Newbigin.

There is, therefore, no compelling reason in the multiplicity of faiths and the number of their adherents to abandon, as Hick does, the finality of Jesus and reduce him to the level of one of the mythical *avatars* of Vishnu.

2. THE OBJECTIONS TO HISTORICAL SCEPTICISM ABOUT JESUS

It is impossible within a few pages to do more than outline some of the difficulties which beset any advanced form of scepticism about the broad historical trustworthiness of the picture of Jesus given us in the New Testament. Three trenchant critiques of this unwarranted scepticism have appeared in recent years: a volume of essays on the historical basis of Christianity edited by Anthony Hanson and entitled *Vindications* (ironically enough, it was published by the S.C.M. Press), Eric Mascall's *The Secularisation of Christianity*, and a legal expert, J. N. D. Anderson's *A Lawyer among the Theologians*. Most recently we have had Howard Marshall's *I Believe in the Historical Jesus* which no serious student of the subject will be able to ignore. At present I shall confine myself to seven observations about sceptical Gospel criticism.

It makes some strange assumptions

The first runs something like this. All the records about Jesus that we have come from after Easter. They are therefore all prejudiced, since their authors wrote from the perspective of the Easter faith. There is an extraordinary logical fallacy within this otherwise rather helpful observation. It is that because the writers believed Jesus was the Messiah, and Son of God, and risen from the dead, these assertions are certainly not true! It is one thing to recognise bias and aim off for it: it is quite another to suppose that because men passionately believe something to be true it must therefore be false. As a matter of fact, the readiness with which many of the sayings of Jesus go back into Aramaic, and the features in his teaching which were without parallel in the teaching of the early Church (such as the use of parables and the title Son of Man) indicate that it is probably not the case that we have in the Gospels no material that antedates the Easter faith. But even if we had none, it would not follow that a single word of the Gospel material was untrustworthy. It might be: it might not be. That would have to be established on quite other criteria.

The second strange assumption advocated by the Form Critics in general and Dennis Nineham in particular is that the early Christians had no interest in history, and that nothing could have survived about Jesus unless it was of significance for the liturgical, evangelistic or apologetic concerns of the Church. But why so extraordinary an assumption? Is it not in the highest degree probable that men and women would want to know what manner of man this Jesus was in whom they were being asked to put their trust? The danger of this type of assumption is that what look like pieces of historical evidence in the Gospels are explained away on other grounds. Thus to take a trivial example, when Mark includes, in his account of the Feeding, that Jesus made the people sit down on the green grass, Nineham in his commentary comments, "It would be a mistake to see in these words evidence of eye-witness recollection" (p.183). It is important to be clear what is happening. We are not being presented with a scholarly conclusion about the historical value of the biblical material before us, but with the assumption of a particular scholar or school of scholars—an assumption we may properly decline to share.

The third surprising assumption is that the early Church made up a great many of the stories in the Gospels and Acts. They did so, we are told, in order to meet their own needs in worship, teaching, preaching and the like. This gratuitous assumption has the great attraction of allowing the scholar to go on examining the meaning of a story to the evangelist without bothering his head about whether or not it actually happened—a sort of literary docetism. But it runs into serious difficulties.

For one thing it attributes enormous creative powers to the nameless 'community' of early Christians who made these stories up. But this is to neglect one of the most obvious facts of life, that committees do not create: when you get vital, forceful stories such as we find galore in the Gospels it is infinitely more probable that they derive from a single commanding character than from some nameless group of Hellenistic Christians. For another, it neglects the fact that the early Christians were not only quite capable of distinguishing between their own teaching and that of Jesus, but that they were meticulous in doing so (see St. Paul in 1 Cor. 7.10 and 25). What is more, if this account of the creative activity of the early Church were correct we should surely expect to find in the stories made up and attributed to Jesus the sort of issues that they themselves were concerned with. Instead, the burning issues of the early Church, such as the Holy Spirit, Baptism, the Eucharist, the Church, Food Laws and Circumcision are conspicuous by their absence. As Professor Richard Hanson has puckishly commented, "Why should this large collection of fictitious material have been composed by a number of anonymous authors within a few years of the death of this person whose existence was historical but about whom we can know nothing else historical in spite of four narratives which purport to tell us about him?' (*Vindication*, p.41.)

It neglects the judgment of ancient historians

One of the unfortunate facts in contemporary Gospel criticism is that not many of those engaged in it have been thoroughly grounded in the discipline of historical study. Few indeed of them are expert in ancient history, let alone ancient historiography. That might not matter so much, maybe, if they listened to those who are expert. But this is just what does not happen. Scepticism about the historical Jesus should come, one might suppose, from the ancient historians. But nothing could be further from the truth. It is the theologians who are willing to dispense with historicity, and it is the historians who are trying to restrain them! Distinguished ancient historians like Ramsay, Rostovtzeff, B. W. Henderson, Sherwin-White are men who ascribe a very high reliability to the New Testament narratives. The same is true of New Testament scholars like Reicke, Stauffer, Dodd, Moule and Bruce who have come to the New Testament via classical studies. In other words, the historical scepticism is not induced by the material but by the presuppositions of sceptical theologians.

Professor Anthony Hanson remarks in *Vindications* (p.89) that "the Nineham treatment will discredit the historical reliablity of *any* document", and by this he means the tendency to discredit any statement that purports to be historical and to seek another meaning for it. Indeed, in the previous pages Hanson has himself applied the "Nineham treatment" with some glee to Josephus' *Bellum Judaicum* and to Tacitus' *Agricola*. Both of these writers were like the evangelists in having a clear overruling idea in writing their books. Fine. But that does not mean that everything they said must be false! The proper historical procedure would be to make due allowance for their bias and then to treat them as reliable unless their account is internally incoherent or factually disapproved.

Sherwin-White draws his book to an end by contrasting the approach of the professional ancient historian and some New Testament scholars. In *Roman Society and Roman Law in the New Testament* (p.187f) he writes:

So it is astonishing that while Graeco-Roman historians have been growing in confidence, the twentieth century study of the Gospel narratives starting from no less promising material, has taken so gloomy a turn in the development of form criticism that the more advanced exponents of it apparently maintain—so far as an amateur can understand them—that the historical Christ is unknowable and the history of his mission cannot be written. This seems very curious when one compares the case for the best-known contemporary of Christ, who like Christ is a well-documented figure—Tiberius Caesar. The story of his reign is known from four sources, the *Annals* of Tacitus and the biography of Suetonius, written some eighty or ninety years later, the brief contemporary record of Velleius Paterculus, and the third-century history of Cassius Dio. These disagree among themselves in the wildest possible fashion, both in major matters of political action or motive and in the specific details of minor events. Everyone would admit that Tacitus is the best of all the sources, and yet no serious modern historian would accept at face value the majority of the statements of Tacitus about the motives of Tiberius. But this does not prevent the belief that the material of Tacitus can be used to write a history of Tiberius. The divergences between the synoptic Gospels, or between them and the Fourth Gospel, are no worse than the contradictions in the Tiberius material.

It fails to take account of the Jewishness of the New Testament

Much of the creativity of the early Church is supposed to have taken place when the gospel moved out from the confines of Judaism on to the soil of the Gentile world. Stories about Jesus were then fashioned, we are led to believe, along the lines of the 'divine men' of paganism, and the myths of Hellenistic culture. This is one of the basic assumptions of the Form Critics. But this approach neglects two vital factors. The first is the retentiveness of the Oriental memory. Many Jews knew the whole of the Pentateuch off by heart: many Greeks could recite the whole Iliad. Teaching in school was done by means of repetition. The sheer power of memory they possessed is hard for us to recapture in the age of the book and the television screen. But it existed, and to discount it is bad scholarship. There are many people alive today who can remember not just the outlines but the main substance of Churchill's war speeches, and the historical situation in which they originated. Are we to suppose that his contemporaries could remember nothing very much of their contemporary, a greater than Churchill, despite the retentiveness of their memories and the fact that the Gospels were written somewhat nearer to the events they describe than we are to the Second World War?

The sheer Jewishness of the New Testament is the second point to bear in mind here. We are not merely pointing to the controlling effect on the vagaries of tradition imposed by the survival of eye-witness, but to the fact that these men were all Jews. The New Testament is not a Hellenistic book. Its greatest affinities lie with Judaism. Jesus was a Jewish rabbi, and the disciples were Jewish to a man. They had been educated in remembering the words of their master, and they were competent in recalling it. This whole point has been made very forcibly by Harald Riesenfeld (*The Gospel Tradition and its Beginnings*) and Birger Gerhardsson (*Memory and Manu-*

script), two Swedish scholars of great ability whose work has been virtually ignored in Germany—it is too uncomfortable. But they have shown beyond the possibility of cavil that the teaching of Jesus, as brought to us in the Gospels, is Jewish through and through, and that to suppose it is the creation of Hellenistic mythopoeic communities is quite gratuitous. W. D. Davies has done the same in establishing the essential Jewishness of St. Paul (*Paul and Rabbinic Judaism*). The fact of the matter is that in the New Testament we are dealing with material that comes from the Jewish core of Jesus and his early associates. W. D. Davies, one of the greatest living experts on the Jewish background to the New Testament, has some strong criticisms to make of the work of Riesenfeld and Gerhardsson, but concludes his review article (*The Setting of the Sermon on the Mount*, p.480) by saying:

> By bringing to bear the usages of contemporary Judaism, in a fresh and comprehensive manner, on the transmission of the Gospel tradition, they have forcibly compelled the recognisation of structural parallels between much in Primitive Christianity and Pharisaic Judaism. This means, in our judgment, that they have made it far more historically probable and reasonably credible, over against the scepticism of much form criticism, that in the Gospels we are within hearing of the authentic voice and within sight of the authentic activity of Jesus of Nazareth.

It frequently makes gross errors in methodology

Very frequently you find sceptical New Testament scholars asserting that if there is any parallel to a Gospel incident in the Old Testament then we must suppose that the Gospel writers created the story, and that it must be discounted. Thus the story of the Temptation of Jesus can be dissolved into the forty years of Israel's wandering in the wilderness, Adam with the wild animals, and Elijah's time of discouragement and sustenance in the desert. Fascinating but entirely imaginary! Why on earth should it not be the case that the high point of Jesus' baptism and assurance of Sonship was followed by a time of wondering about this vocation and testing it out against other possibilities in the loneliness of the desert? There is nothing in the story to suggest unreliability; there is much in the scholarly reconstruction to suggest bias.

Very frequently you find sceptical New Testament scholars comparing New Testament stories about Jesus to Norse and Homeric legends. The comparison is not altogether felicitous, as those who are skilled in Norse and Homeric sagas recognise. One of the experts most at home in this type of literature was the Oxford English don, C. S. Lewis. He comments robustly in *Christian Reflections*:

> I have been reading poems, romances, vision literature, legends, myths all my life. I know what they are like. I know that none of them is like this. Of this text there are only two possible views. Either this is reportage—though it may no doubt contain errors—pretty close up to the facts; nearly as close as Boswell. Or else, some unknown writer in the second century, without known predecessors or successors, suddenly anticipated the whole technique of modern, novelistic, realistic narrative. If it is untrue, it must be narrative of that kind. The reader who doesn't see this simply has not learned to read.

> I myself studied Homeric Archaeology at Oxford. And I know that the experts in the subject are altogether more willing to allow the material to teach them what happened in the days of the Trojan War than some New Testament scholars are to allow the Gospels to teach them what happened in the life and work of Jesus. This is all the more astonishing when you consider the time gap. The Homeric poems were probably first written down in the

late sixth century, but they contain material dating back a thousand years before that, and come at the end of a period of oral transmission almost as long. But with the New Testament we are in an entirely different situation. The oral period is a mere thirty years or so, and the controlling influence of eyewitness is still a major factor in the tradition. The analogy with Homeric myths is one of the most inept to have been foisted upon New Testament studies.

Very frequently you find sceptical New Testament scholars asserting that if any story in the Gospels has a parallel in the Old Testament, or in rabbinic Judaism, or in the Hellenistic world, or in the life of the early Church it must be discounted. This criterion is laid out with disarming naïvety by R. H. Fuller in *The Foundations of New Testament Christology*, p.18, and though widespread, it is absolutely laughable. How often do you say anything which is utterly original and for which no parallel can be found among the literature you read, the friends you have, the society you live in, and any pupils you may gather round you?

This 'criterion of dissimilarity' as it is called, assumes we know enough about what could have been said by the early Church or contemporary Judaism to distinguish it with certainty from the teaching of Jesus. The fact is that we do not. This principle, if rigorously applied, would rule out all continuity between the Teacher and his disciples; it would mean that nothing Jesus taught them stuck! This principle could, even if it were in principle operable, only give us what is unique in the teaching of Jesus, which might not be the main thrust of his teaching at all, and might lead to a very distorted picture of him. It is a tool which is not without some value but needs to be used with very great caution. Professor Morna Hooker comments aptly, "To be acceptable as genuine a saying of Jesus must at the same time be 'dissimilar' from contemporary Judaism, and yet use its categories and reflect the language and style of Aramaic. In òther words, authentic sayings must not be reflected in Judaism (as far as it is known to us) but must sound as if they could have been spoken at that time" (*New Testament Studies*, 17, p.482).

Yes, there are frequent methodological errors in the procedures of the sceptics.

It has a curious preference for inferior evidence

Take the *theios anēr* motif which we have already discussed. There is among many New Testament scholars a quite uncritical readiness to imagine that *theioi andres* were two a penny in antiquity. The evidence we have concerning the best known of them, Apollonius of Tyana, comes from the end of the second century! And yet we are often asked to believe that the story of Jesus was fashioned on exemplars such as this.

Take the influence of the mystery cults. It is still widely held, particularly among sceptical German theologians, that Christian sacramental theology is based on communion with a dying and rising deity such as we find in some of the mystery cults. But quite apart from the fact that similarity would not prove borrowing (and the early Christians showed no sign of syncretism with the mystery religions), the date for all this material is firmly post-Christian. Recently Lloyd Geering has revived this theory (destroyed by Kennedy more than a generation ago) and has suggested that the resurrection of Jesus on the third day was derived from the cult of Attis and Adonis. Quite apart from the inherent improbability of such a derivation (the earliest disciples were Jews), the evidence for the 'resurrection' of either Attis or Adonis cannot be traced back further than the end of the second century A.D. by which time conscious efforts were being made to revive paganism as a counterbalance to the growth of Christianity.

Take the Gnostic Redeemer Myth. How often we meet him in the writings of New Testament scholars who are unhappy about the incarnation and ascension. And how rarely do they have the honesty that Frances Young displays in her chapter in the symposium to admit that there is no evidence whatever for this supposed Gnostic Redeemer in any pre-Christian material. And if there was, that would not for one moment invalidate the possibility that God did become man in order to redeem us. Analogy cannot invalidate history.

Take the Acts of the Apostles. In just a couple of places there may be contiguity between Luke and Josephus, the Jewish historian who wrote at the end of the first century. It is well known that Josephus was tendentious and at times highly unreliable. Yet sceptical New Testament scholars regularly prefer his version to that of Luke, who has repeatedly been shown, to the satisfaction of Roman historians, to be remarkably accurate in the picture he presents of first-century society. If Luke and Josephus clash (and it is by no means certain that they do) why should it be Luke who gets the thick end of the stick?

Or take the authorship of the Fourth Gospel. There is strong and very early evidence that John the apostle of the Lord wrote the Fourth Gospel. Many modern scholars do not think he did. So what do they do? They try to explain away the powerful evidence of Irenaeus, and his personal link with John through Polycarp, and prefer the evidence of a ninth-century monk, George the Sinner (who was doubtless not given his nickname for nothing). If sceptical scholars would show the same scepticism towards the sources they want to follow as those which they do not want to follow, the cause of truth would be advanced.

It cannot believe that history matters

The current flight from history among theologians, in contrast to historians, is a curious phenomenon. It may have many causes, but among them these three certainly figure prominently.

First, there is fear. Fear that historical discovery might

spoil Christian belief. Ever since Schleiermacher there has been a strain within Christendom which has tried to preserve Christianity from exposure to the vicissitudes of historical and scientific research. But this fear must be resisted. We must have the courage to say, "If history or science disproves the Christian proclamation, the quicker we give it up the better."

Second, there is unbelief. Unbelief that the contingencies of history could have anything to do with the assurance of faith. This problem goes back to Lessing, who claimed that "accidental truths of history can never become the proof of necessary truths of reason". Howard Marshall's comments on this are exceedingly to the point (*op. cit.* p.104–6). In the first place, the Christian religion is not based on any attempt to derive "necessary truths of reason" from history. It is concerned with historical events which can be seen as instruments of divine revelation and redemption. And if you reformulate Lessing's dictum to mean that you cannot accept the claim to divine revelation and redemption through historical events which are themselves in doubt, the answer must be that this is precisely what we are being challenged to do. The incarnation is the supreme example of "that which could have been otherwise". It is historically contingent: but what else could it be? All historical events could have been otherwise. The Christian claim is that the evidence supporting belief in the incarnation of God is more than strong enough and many-sided enough to warrant faith. As Marshall points out, "the strength of the historical argument for Christianity is that of a piece of chain mail rather than that of a single chain". There are so many historical evidences involved that even if some of them are uncertain it does not disturb the reliability of others. We have seen something of this in the very varied testimony to the deity of Jesus in the New Testament evidence adduced in Chapter 1. And Lessing's unwillingness to commit himself unless persuaded of the strength of all the links in the chain-mail suit is perverse. He is quite willing to commit himself in the basis of his own observation, he tells us. But that observation may be much less reliable than ancient testimony from others. Indeed, as Kierkegaard pointed out in his *Philosophical Fragments*, we have a great deal more historical evidence about Jesus than we strictly need. If all that had survived from the circle of the disciples was the testimony that Jesus, through his person, teaching and resurrection had brought God into their midst, and that in trusting their lives to him they had not been let down—that would have sufficed to challenge future generations to make the same experiment of faith. In point of fact, of course, we are infinitely richer than that, with the four Gospels which have come down to us from the early Church.

The third root of the cavalier attitude to history displayed by many modern New Testament writers is the desire to safeguard justification by faith. This is pre-eminently a Lutheran concern, and many of the foremost sceptical scholars are, like Bultmann himself, Lutherans. He maintains that the faith which justifies must be alone, and to prop it up with history is to render it no longer faith. There is something in this, but frankly, not much. It owes a good deal to Bultmann's own existentialist understanding of faith as self-awareness and openness to the future. But faith does not mean that, either in the Bible or in popular usage. It means self-commitment on evidence. It is thus that we display our faith in a doctor, in a marriage partner, or in Christ. Faith is not blind. It is based on evidence and directed towards an object thought to be worthy. In the case of Christian faith it arose for the earliest disciples from historical contemporaneity with Jesus. They were not *compelled* by the evidence: plenty of people saw it and declined to commit themselves. But the evidence was the ground on which they committed themselves; it seemed to them to justify self-commitment. They committed themselves, and discovered that life with

Christ was a reality. With later generations it is much the same. We do not have the witness of our eyes to go on: in any case, if we judged according to appearances we could be very wrong, as many of Jesus' contemporaries were. Instead we have the witness of those earliest believers. They tell us that they believed and found Christ to be as good as his word: they also tell us why they believed, and the evidence that convinced them is brought before us in the Gospels. It remains more than enough to warrant (though never to compel) commitment. The integrity of faith is maintained: it is my trusting, adoring, self-commitment to the Lord who has loved me and died for me. But the place of history is no less necessary: it is on the witness of those early disciples to what they saw and heard and experienced that I take this step of commitment. Encounter is always based on evidence. If you want a Christianity that is impervious to historical evidence and the scrutiny of historical research, that is just too bad. Christianity is about a God who has immersed himself in history, and a non-historical version is not Christianity at all but Hinduism. For history does matter. God created us in history. God is the sovereign governor of history. God became incarnate in history. God redeemed us in history. God's purpose for his world is historical, though it transcends history: we are offered no escape of the soul to the beyond, as in Eastern religions and the mystery cults, but a resurrection of the body in a redeemed community in the heavenly city. In a word, remove history from the Christian faith, and it ceases to be Christianity at all. And the tendencies of *The Myth of God Incarnate* are strongly in this direction.

It produces schizoid men

Christian salvation both means and produces wholeness. But couple historical scepticism with a Christian profession and it tears a man apart. This is very evident in that distinguished New Testament scholar, Rudolf Bultmann. He was orthodox Lutheran enough to believe that the proclamation of the gospel in preaching must not be questioned by the hearers: it should challenge them to decision. You don't argue with it: you respond to it. But Bultmann the sceptical scholar conceded merely the historical existence and crucifixion of Jesus and believed that Jesus was nothing but the bare presupposition of Christian proclamation. Between Bultmann the preacher on Sundays and Bultmann the scholar on Mondays a great gulf was fixed. It was a gulf that was never satisfactorily bridged. Some of his followers went over to atheism. Some of them started a new quest for the historical Jesus.

One of the English scholars most influenced by Bultmann is a contributor to the symposium, Dennis Nineham. He must answer for himself, but he gives the appearance of also being a very divided man. I have heard him so expound the Gospels that you would imagine that he believed every word of it. Yet I have heard him maintain that even if we could know anything for certain of Jesus' teachings he would not consider it binding on him as a Christian. Professor Anthony Hanson has done some research on the divide between Nineham the critic and Nineham the preacher in *Vindications*, p.90ff. He points out how wide a gulf separates Dr. Nineham's critical work from his devotional teaching. In a series of three articles in the *Journal of Theological Studies* on eyewitness testimony and the Gospel tradition, Nineham treats the incident of the paralytic man let down through the roof to Jesus in Mark 2.1–10 as unhistorical, whereas in his *A New Way of Looking at the Gospels*, a popular monograph, he treats the incident as history. In the same book, which originated as broadcast talks, he accepts the fact that Jesus used Isaiah 53 to describe his mission; but in a scholarly review in *Theology* (March 1956) he scouts the idea. "The only conclusion I can draw," writes Hanson, after reviewing these and other contradictions, "from this remarkable contrast between Nineham the critic and

Nineham the preacher is that in fact his critical pre-suppositions do not leave him enough on which to base a true devotion to the Word incarnate, and that therefore when he is writing devotionally he has to assume more than his assumptions otherwise permit him. This puts a large question mark against his own solution to the quandary of historical scepticism." He goes on to examine and criticise Dr. Nineham's own solution, which revolves round two assumptions, that we have enough historical knowledge of Jesus for our purpose as Christians, and that we must trust the Church for the rest.

Things have moved on in three respects since Hanson wrote this appraisal in 1966. In his present contribution of an Epilogue to *The Myth of God Incarnate* we find Dr. Nineham taking to task the other contributors to that volume for continuing to seek some uniqueness for Jesus after abandoning belief in his literal incarnation. He quite rightly points out that on their premises no ground for such a claim exists. Historical enquiry by itself cannot even in principle give them the results they are looking for. "The aim of the present postscript has been to put a 'No thoroughfare' against any alternative routes which may be suggested by way of claiming uniqueness of some sort for Jesus on historical grounds" (p.201). Secondly, it would appear that he has abandoned devotion to the Word incarnate. For the Jesus he is advocating is not now seen as the Word incarnate at all. And in the third place, how are we to trust the Church to guide us aright on matters where historical evidence fails us? The Church, through its recognition of the canonical Gospels, through its Apostles' and Nicene Creeds, through its Chalcedonian and countless other definitions has guided us, and Dr. Nineham is taking leave to depart from that guidance. It can hardly be claimed that historical scepticism of this nature makes for integrated thinking and living.

3. THE CONSEQUENCES OF SCEPTICISM ABOUT THE HISTORICAL INCARNATION

It is greatly to the credit of several of the writers in the symposium that they seek to examine some of the consequences that might follow if their account of the 'myth' of God incarnate is in fact correct. But I do not believe that they have been nearly rigorous enough. Here are seven consequences which would seem to follow if God did not become man in Jesus Christ, but that the story that he did so is a 'myth'.

No knowledge of God

First, God would become once again the unknown God. One of the great things about the incarnation was that it made God not only knowable but known. In Christ he had disclosed enough of himself for us to be getting along with. "God is Christlike, and in him is no un-Christlikeness at all" was Michael Ramsey's way of putting the matter. But if there is no ontological relationship between God and Jesus of Nazareth, how are we to be sure that the Jesus myth is at all appropriate for helping us to understand what God is like? Why should we not turn to one of the Hindu *avatars*? The authors of this symposium believe in God. They believe he is loving. They believe he is fatherlike. But how do they arrive at such remarkable conclusions? On logical grounds, there is no way in which they can do so. They in fact achieve it by connotation language. They are still using the coinage of Christian language when they have made it worthless overnight. If there is no incarnation, how can I know that God is love? Looking at all the pain and sorrow in the world, why should I not assume that he is a monster—if indeed he is personal at all? The only way we used to know was through God actually entering into our agony and loss and alienation through the incarnation. Now all that turns out to be a pleasing but insubstantial myth. I may claim to remain a theist, like the authors of the symposium, but I shall worship the unknown God who has not given me a revelation of himself that necessarily corresponds to his real nature. And for all their attempts to distinguish their position from old-fashioned Unitarianism, I shall have to confess myself unable to discern the difference.

No atonement

Another of the wonders of the incarnation was the fact that it made possible the atonement. Not only did God deign to show me what he was like in terms I could understand, the terms of a human life: but he deigned to bridge the gap between my unworthiness and his holiness. The cross formed that bridge. It was on the cross that we used to believe, in the old days, that God had visited and redeemed his people. It was on the cross that he took personal responsibility for our wickedness and let our sins crush him. It was on the cross that he suffered our pain and died our death. He had not just told us a 'myth', a lovely poetic story about sacrificial love, but had demonstrated it to the uttermost. If the incarnation spelt God's revelation to man, the atonement spelt God's reconciliation of man.

But we have grown out of all that now. We are men come of age, and we do not need the crudities of history any more. We are nourished on myth. So be it. But no myth can reconcile the sinner to the Holy One. If God was in Christ, reconciling the world to himself, I can take it in—just: in awe and wonder, and deep, joyful gratitude. But if it is a 'myth', however poetic and ennobling, I remain as alienated from God as ever I did. No incarnation involves the corollary of no atonement.

No resurrection

The whole of Christian optimism about the future has

been built on the actual, historical resurrection of Jesus Christ from the dead. That is the only assurance we have that the death of Christ availed to reconcile us. That is the only evidence we have of our own resurrection from death. That is the only solid hope we have for God's future. Without that resurrection of Jesus, all talk of heaven is so much pie in the sky; it merits Bertrand Russell's gibe about Christianity, that belief in fairy tales is pleasant.

I used to believe that there was a future for mankind, both individually and corporately. That assurance was based on the resurrection of Jesus. But now I realise that I was misled by the literalists and fundamentalists who could not distinguish poetry from prose. Now I appreciate that the story of the incarnation is a myth, and therefore that the resurrection is a myth also, a delightful symbol of hope without a shred of evidence to support its truth. But I am man come of age: I now fully recognise the mythical nature of it all and "draw on the resources of the faith more richly" as one of the essayists put it. But what was that I remember from long ago in the days when I used to read the New Testament? "If the dead are not raised, then Christ has not been raised. If Christ has not been raised your faith is futile and you are still in your sins. Those also who have fallen asleep in Christ have perished. If for this life only we have hoped in Christ, we are of all men most to be pitied."

No Holy Spirit

The Holy Spirit does not seem to have qualified for much of a mention in this symposium, but inevitably we must now bid him farewell. He was there all right (albeit for centuries given only lip-service) in the old days of trinitarian theology, when we used to believe that love was at the heart of the universe, and that love involved diversity within unity at the heart of the Godhead. He became available, so they used to say, through the incarnation, resurrection and ascension of Jesus, because the

Spirit of God was fully personalised in Jesus and thereafter released into the lives of believers. That was what conversion and the new birth and all those old fashioned notions were about. It was supposed to mean that a new quality of life was made available to the believer. But we cannot believe in conversion any more in these multi-faith days. As for the new birth, it is either mere symbolism (baptism) or mere emotionalism (conversion). The Spirit of God may have dimmed somewhat, but no matter: the spirit of man is burning all the brighter.

No sacraments

In the old days sacraments used to be seen as not merely earthly actions with spiritual meanings, but the spiritual embodied in the physical. They were extending the principle of the incarnation. But now that the physical involvement of the divine in our world is discredited, now that Jesus is seen to be only mythically not metaphysically the Son of God, we shall have to give up taking the sacraments of the Church in any realistic sense. No longer can they embody the Beyond in our midst. But perhaps that is just as well. After all, the Beyond has not come into the midst, so let us cease pretending that he has.

It is a long cry from the transubstantiation of those benighted men in the middle ages, and even further from that Jewish rabbi who was reputed, but of course apocryphally, to have said, "Truly, truly I say to you, unless you eat the flesh of the Son of man and drink his blood, you have no life in you." Let's be consistent then. We will remain Christians, of course: we have adapted the word to our understanding of it. But we may as well do without the sacraments, like the Quakers and the Salvation Army. It's a funny thing, but I always used to think they were missing out on something.

No message

Of course I still have a message, now that I understand

that the incarnation is a myth. It is a much more imaginative and flexible message, and far better able to contain contradictions than the old one. It is a sublime story, the most wonderful ever told—at least, that is how I think of it. But naturally, the Hindu may prefer his own version, and the Muslim may perhaps be quite exclusive about his. No matter, I shall tell men this story, and I may perhaps add from time to time that it didn't, of course, actually happen. But wouldn't it have been wonderful if it had?

I will not expect my hearers necessarily to make a great deal of use of the Bible. We have in any case revised it fairly extensively these days, and it is now much more compact. But there are many holy books, and it does not much matter which one men use or which myth they adopt. We are all going up the same mountain, albeit by different routes. Or are some going down?

No Christianity

Of course I can still say the creeds, and I do, but I prefer to sing them, and then I don't feel that I am expected to mean what I am saying . . . or singing. It is just a question of theological sophistication. Actually, there is nothing new or shocking about this mythical understanding of Jesus. It is very much what the early Christians were trying to say, but they lacked the philosophical, linguistic and theological tools which are now happily available to us. Christianity is now entering a new phase in its long history of "adapting itself to what can be believed". It is already virtually indistinguishable from humanism and Hinduism, and will soon become the undifferentiated world religion we are all looking for, which will embrace all the myths of all the peoples in the—hopefully real—heavenly home of the one God and Father of us all.

POSTSCRIPT

Christianity without Incarnation?
Some Critical Comments

John Macquarrie

THE SENSATIONAL TITLE of this book* is unfortunate, for it will no doubt provoke an emotive reaction, especially among those who do not trouble to read the actual text. It may at once be agreed that the story of a divine being who descends to earth as man is technically a 'myth' and not a straightforward history, though one of the troubles of this book is that its writers waver between a critique of the *myth* of incarnation and the *metaphysics* of incarnation, and quite a bit of confusion arises from the failure to distinguish these two problems.

The book is a serious discussion by seven scholars as to whether the idea of incarnation can still have in Christian faith the place given to it in the past. The authors are correct in saying that "there is nothing new in the main theme of this book"—indeed, those readers who have some acquaintance with the history of Christian thought may find that much of it conveys the impression of *déjà vu.*

* This is a slightly revised version of a review written for *Theology* of *The Myth of God Incarnate*, ed. John Hick (S.C.M., 1977).

At least since the time of Schleiermacher, systematic theologians have criticised the traditional Christology on many grounds—the confusion of the terminology, the remoteness of the concepts from modern thought, the obscuring of the humanity of Christ, and so on. But the present book takes little note of systematic theology, being mainly historical in orientation. Michael Goulder, for instance, spends much time and ingenuity in trying to show that incarnation was an idea taken over from the Samaritans, and he seems to think that this is enough to discredit it—surely an almost perfect illustration of the genetic fallacy. There is hardly any mention in the book as a whole of the constructive insights of such contemporary writers as Pannenberg, Rahner, Schoonenberg, Kasper, von Balthasar and others, all of whom are quite aware of the difficulties raised in the book, but have not thought it necessary to reject the idea of incarnation and have tried to rethink it in a broader and modern context of Christological interpretation.

A defect of the book is the failure to use terms consistently and, more generally, to attend to the peculiarities of religious and theological language, especially its oblique and sometimes paradoxical character. Leslie Houlden does in fact make a beginning towards a discussion of language, but his eight-page essay is too brief to take us very far. The general failure to come to grips with the language problem may be illustrated from an essay by Frances Young. She writes: "There are strong reasons for seeing the patristic development and interpretation of incarnational belief not as a gradual dawning of the truth inspired by the Holy Spirit but as a historically determined development which led into the blind alleys of paradox, illogicality and docetism." But when she comes to expound her own robust (if almost purely functional) faith in Christ, she tells us that we have to live with unresolved contradictions and even that "religion is destroyed without mystery—without paradox". What makes her paradoxes acceptable rather than the patristic ones?

Incidentally, the talk about patristic thought being 'historically determined' expresses an attitude that is found elsewhere in the book, for instance, in Leslie Houlden's statement that "we must accept our lot, bequeathed to us by the Enlightenment, and make the most of it". If our thinking at any given time is so strictly determined by the prevailing historical and cultural conditions, does not this imply a scepticism that is eventually self-destroying and takes away the possibility of rational discrimination and new departures of thought?

But to come back to the main theme, consistency in the use of the key term 'myth' would seem to be important, but it is not until one is three quarters of the way through the book that the term is discussed in detail by Maurice Wiles, and, as he points out, it has already been freely used in the earlier chapters. His own discussion is clarifying and helpful, but it surely calls in question the looseness of usage that can be found in other parts of the book. The very first use of the term 'myth' occurs in the Preface, where we read: " 'Orthodoxy' is a myth, which can and often does inhibit the creative thinking which Christianity sorely needs today." What does 'myth' mean here? Are we to take it in its technical sense, to mean that 'orthodoxy' is expressed in the form of mythological stories? If so, the statement is clearly false, for much 'orthodoxy' is conceptually expressed in dogmatic definitions. Or are we (which seems more likely) to take 'myth' in its popular sense as something merely false, so that the assertion, " 'Orthodoxy' is a myth" means: "It is false that there is an unchanging body of propositions called 'orthodoxy' "? If this second interpretation is correct, so that 'myth' is being used in much the same sense as the word 'mirage' used two sentences earlier, then it is surely inexcusable that in a serious work the key term 'myth' should be introduced for the first time in its loosest popular sense.

There are problems too in the use of the term 'incarnation'. One of the contributors wants to reject a 'literal incarnation doctrine', but it is not clear, given the oblique character of theological language, what a 'literal' incarnation could mean. Another contributor seems nearer the mark when he says that literal and metaphorical are not distinguishable in the talk of incarnation and that the doctrine is "not a theory but a mystery". It is an image, rather than a concept. Still, it is an image that tries to express some things about Jesus Christ that may not be expressed or may not be so clearly expressed by other images, such as Messiah or Lord or Liberator or whatever.

I would think that *at least* three things are implied in the idea of incarnation: (a) the initiative is from God, not man; (b) God is deeply involved in his creation; (c) the centre of this initiative and involvement is Jesus Christ.

Obviously, some of these points are accepted by some of the contributors to the book, and to that extent I would say that they are assenting to at least part of what many Christians would understand by incarnation. For example, Frances Young appears to accept (a) and Leslie Houlden (b). Don Cupitt might have a problem with these two points, because he emphasises so much the transcendence of God and has an iconoclastic horror of representing God by anything or anyone in the created order. His critique of incarnation is in fact very telling if one understands the doctrine as the exaltation of a human being to deity, but it loses its force if one thinks of the movement as from the opposite direction, as Barth did in his teaching about the humanity of God. All the contributors would give some assent to (c), for even if they do not allow that Christ is God incarnate, they do acknowledge that he has an important place in the history of God's relation to mankind. Maurice Wiles, however, seems to lean to the old idealist belief that Jesus is simply the historical exemplar of the timeless truth of the unity of God and man.

The contributors to the book are united in their dissatisfaction with traditional doctrines of incarnation, but they have no common reconstruction of belief to offer. Inevitably, therefore, the impression produced is negative and reductionist. According to Maurice Wiles, the abandonment of the doctrine of incarnation "would not involve the abandonment of all the religious claims associated with it". But we are entitled to ask: "If not *all* the claims, then which ones?" Christian doctrines are so closely interrelated that if you take away one, several others tend to collapse. After incarnation is thrown out, is the doctrine of the Trinity bound to go? What kind of doctrine of atonement remains possible? Would the Eucharist be reduced simply to a memorial service? What a rewriting of creeds and liturgies, of prayer books and hymn books, even of Holy Scripture, would be demanded!

Finally, one has to ask whether such a reduced Christianity would move us either to acceptance or rejection. No doubt it would survive as literature, but hardly as a living religious faith. It would be an anachronism to describe the positions in this book as Arian, deist or Unitarian, but unquestionably there are affinities, and it is hardly likely that an updated Christianity without incarnation will prove any more successful than these dead ends of the past.